Focal Points:

Focal Points:

Nancy Spero

Robert Storr

Edited by Francesca Pietropaolo

HENI Publishing, London

ISBN 978-1-911736-34-9

Cover: Nancy Spero
The Bug, Helicopter, Victim, from the *War Series*, 1966
Gouache and ink on paper, 48.3 × 59.1 cm (19 × 23 ¼ in.)
Pennsylvania Academy of the Fine Arts, Philadelphia.
John S. Phillips Art Fund
Photo courtesy Galerie Lelong, New York
See plate 8

Editor: Francesca Pietropaolo
Designer: Sylvia Ugga
Printed by Toppan Leefung in China

Publisher: HENI Publishing, London, United Kingdom
EU Authorised Representative: Easy Access System Europe -
Mustamäe tee 50, 10621 Tallinn, Estonia
gpsr.requests@easproject.com

Contents

7 Still, like air, I will rise
Francesca Pietropaolo

17 Notes on Nancy
Robert Storr

25 Peripheral Visions

33 Nancy Spero: Central Issues – Peripheral Visions

47 The Weapon and the Wound

59 Plates

137 Author Biographies

141 Acknowledgements

143 Index

Still, like air, I will rise

by Francesca Pietropaolo

This book is devoted to the American painter, collage and installation artist Nancy Spero. Among the most influential practitioners of her generation, over the course of five decades—from her coming of age in the late 1950s–early 1960s through the 2000s—Spero (1926–2009) gave birth to a richly complex body of work that defies easy categorization. Published to coincide with the centenary of her birth, this volume is the fifth in the ongoing *Focal Points* series gathering selected writings by Robert Storr on the work of a single artist or on a critical theme. In it, the American critic illuminates the norm-breaking and open-ended quality of Spero's oeuvre, underlying its ability to embrace contradiction. Favoring experimentation throughout her trajectory, the artist exploded hierarchies among media—painting, drawing, collage, printing, and installation—and dichotomies between the hand-made and the photo-mechanical, power and fragility, the permanent and the ephemeral. As Storr underscores in his introduction in these pages, the measure of her innovative contribution to contemporary art still awaits to be fully taken in.

Profusely illustrated, *Focal Points: Nancy Spero* brings together, for the first time, the critic's writings on the artist—three texts, two of which dating from the late 1980s and one from the early 2000s—where he offers insightful meditations on the approach through which Spero was able to expand the possibilities of art into uncharted territory. As a painter, she relentlessly pushed the boundaries of the medium and, breaking away from the notion of the self-contained rectangular picture plane, starting in the 1970s she developed a new form of pictorial art that increasingly attained a mural scale, allowing for an active dialogue with the architectural space where it is presented—a hybrid practice comprising hand printing, gouache, and collage (of images as well as of typed text) on paper and eventually also printing directly onto the wall in ephemeral installations. A prominent figure in the feminist movement of the 1960s and 1970s, and a vocal activist on pressing political, cultural, and social issues, since the 1970s she created scroll-like works where Woman is the universal protagonist. These are made pasting sheets of paper end to end, a procedure inspired by "Egyptian hieroglyphics—their methods of composition on walls and papyrus," as the artist has recalled.[1] In them, Spero gives life to a vocabulary all her own producing careful compositions in which text and image juxtapose, and figure and ground—that is, the white space of the paper support or of the wall itself—activate each other.

Her art explores history and mythology, language and body, female sexuality, violence, and war, from a unique "place" where fragility and rebellion meet. In the process, it effectively subverts received notions of time, space, and representation.

Finding inspiration in a wide range of sources—both visual and literary—across time, cultures, and geographies, and appropriating them, Spero gives central stage to women's previously silenced voice, to their anger and frustration at being pushed at the margins—the margins of culture, of society, of the art world—as exemplified by her monumental, multi-panel work *Notes in Time* (1976–79; **plates 38–40**). In it, among the many women protagonists, one can find the evocative image of the Greek goddess Artemis who heals women's pain, juxtaposed to an Aztec quote (translated from Nahuatl): "Certainly childbirth is our mortality, we who are women, for it is our battle" (**plate 50**). In exploring the condition of women through mythology and history, Spero keeps her eye firmly on the present, on history in the making. Encapsulating the unique sense of presentness that underlies her transhistorical approach, the artist has remarked: "I try, in everything I do—from using the ancient texts, to the mythological goddesses, to H.D.'s poems on *Helen of Egypt*—to show that it all has reverberations for us today."[2] With intense expressiveness, her art denounces the violence and the discrimination perpetrated against women, past and present, bespeaking their pain as victims; and yet, it retains a sense of hope for

1 Nancy Spero quoted in Jon Bird, "Nancy Spero: Inscribing Woman – Between the Line," in *Nancy Spero* (Institute of Contemporary Art, London, 1987), p.24. Among the parallels that can be drawn, Spero's scroll format is also indebted to East Asian scrolls, the Bayeux Tapestry, and ancient Greek and Roman architectural friezes.

2 Nancy Spero quoted in Jo-Anna Isaak, "Interview: Jo-Anna Isaak in Conversation with Nancy Spero" in Jon Bird et al. *Nancy Spero* (Phaidon, London, 1996), p.24.

the future. In his 1987 essay "Nancy Spero: Central Issues – Peripheral Visions," Storr notes: "Delving in the past while simultaneously speculating on the future course of her society and the possibilities of her medium, Spero's has been and is an art of 'recovery'—and always an art of resistance."[3]

Her politically engaged art does not fall prey to one-dimensional dogmatism or didacticism. Instead, it opens up to a dialogical dimension, a plurality of voices. A polyphonic multitude of women and viewpoints take life in the "stories in fragments" that populate her oeuvre—in a blend of repetition and variation—in compositions that forever subvert the notion of linear narrative—despite the extended linear formats of her installations, both horizontally and vertically.[4] As Storr remarks in his 1987 *Parkett* article "Peripheral Visions," her scroll-like works counter the viewer's expectation for linear narrative and invite an experience of "active visual and intellectual engagement."[5] As he notes, "to follow the complex detail and grasp the complex syntax of a given series of these pictorial fragments one must constantly readjust one's gaze, jumping from one extreme of vision to another and then back to images too hastily scanned in the process."[6]

Furthermore, the viewer of her art is confronted with a richly contradictory universe where unbearable pain and joyful self-celebration co-exist. Spero's work enacts what Storr aptly describes as "a drama of carnal torment, rebellion, and celebration. In it, women struggle against the violence done to them, parade their vitality, and mock the authorities that would confine them to their rhetorical 'place.'"[7]

3 Robert Storr, "Nancy Spero: Central Issues – Peripheral Visions," in the present book, p.46.

4 In the 1970s, Spero began transferring her hand-painted figures to zinc plates. This allowed her to easily reproduce them and repeat them in unrestricted ways. This was a breakthrough allowing for great freedom of invention in her compositions, through repetition and variation of forms and motifs. Repetition also becomes a means for Spero to challenge Western subjectivity. As she explained in a 1985 statement, her works with woman as protagonist "are distanced from the westernized notions of the personal subjective portrayal of individuality... I am not interested in individual physiognomies or personifications... The repetition de-individualizes Western 'subjectivity' in a non-hierarchical continuous presence." Nancy Spero quoted in *Codex Spero: Nancy Spero – Selected Writings and Interviews, 1950–2008*, edited by Roel Arkesteijn (Roma Publications, Amsterdam, 2008) p.115.

5 Robert Storr, "Peripheral Visions," in the present book, p.30.

6 Ibid., p.30.

7 Ibid., p.29.

A member of the cultural and artistic milieu that often gathered at the New York loft that Spero shared with her husband, the American painter Leon Golub (1922–2004), Storr was first introduced to the importance of their work back in his student years as a painter at the School of the Art Institute of Chicago (SAIC), where he completed his Master of Fine Arts degree in 1978, and where both Spero and Golub had previously studied—the couple had left a lasting impact in the Chicago artistic community when they left the city in the late 1950s, heading first to Europe and then to New York. In 2009, in a tribute remembering Spero after her passing, Storr recalls: "[Nancy and Leon] were exceptionally generous to younger artists [whom] they welcomed to their studio, listened to and challenged in conversation, and helped to find outlets for their own work and the means to voice their own commitments. Starting in the early 1980s (I met Golub at an opening in Chicago in 1977 and knew both his and Spero's work well before that) I was lucky to be among them."[8]

As a critic and curator based in New York, from the 1980s onward Storr followed closely the couple's respective work. In 1982 he started contributing to *Art in America* (where he would continue to write regularly until the 2010s) and during that decade, when he came of age as a critic in the New York art world and then internationally, he often wrote on the work of women artists: notable examples include reviews for *Art in America* of exhibitions on Alice Neel, Susan Rothenberg, and Ruth Vollmer, and articles on Louise Bourgeois, Nancy Graves, and Yvonne Rainer. Furthermore, in 1984, Storr inaugurated with an article on Susan Rothenberg his long-standing collaboration with *Art Press* (Paris)—it was the French translation of the article "Spooks and Floats," which had appeared in *Art in America* in May the previous year. Devoted to a woman artist, Elizabeth Murray, was also his first article for *Parkett* (Zurich) published in 1986—he would go on contributing to the magazine through the early 2010s. It is in this context that two of the texts in this book were produced, the *Parkett* article "Peripheral Visions" and the essay "Nancy Spero: Central Issues – Peripheral

8 Robert Storr, "A Tribute to Nancy Spero," *The Brooklyn Rail* (November 2009): https://brooklynrail.org/2009/11/art/a-tribute-to-nancy-spero-1926-2009/Testament?" in the present book, p.23.

Visions" (both from 1987), the latter originally written for the exhibition catalogue *Nancy Spero: Works Since 1950*. In these writing pieces, Storr discusses the development of Spero's trajectory from her figurative paintings of the late 1950s to the works on paper known as the *Artaud Paintings* (1969–70; **plates 22–27**), to her seminal scroll-like works *Codex Artaud* (1971–72; **plates 28–29, 30–31, 32, 33, 34**) and *Notes in Time* (1976–79; **plates 38–54**), to *The First Language* (1981; **plates 55–56**) and *Vietnamese Women* (1985; **plates 62–63**) which were recent works at the time of his writing.

In particular, in his *Parkett* article, Storr reflects on how in the 1980s Spero's work tended to be labeled as "feminist" to isolating effect: "Known as a 'feminist'—which she most certainly is, but which label has become a primary means of isolating and so disregarding her achievement—Spero, now in her sixties, is notable for her stamina and her stubborn refusal to be boxed in by stylistic, ideological or generational labels."[9]

Since her beginnings, the artist demonstrated a relentless impulse to disavow prevailing artistic trends. A case in point is the 1958 oil-on-canvas *Homage to New York (I Do Not Challenge)* (**plate 1**). In it, a large phallic tombstone trophies the initials of the then prevailing Abstract Expressionists—while several of them were women, it was without question a male-dominated art world. The tombstone is flanked by two heads with dunce caps and rabbit-like ears, sticking their tongues out. Suggesting the irreverence of graffiti-like writing, the artist wrote, "I do not challenge" at the top of the image, and, at the bottom, "Homage to New York." In between these texts, she inserted her signature in capital letters, reclaiming her space as an artist. Mocking and anger, defiant laughter and pain blend in this work—the pain of exclusion, as she was then invisible as an artist.

A rejection of Abstract Expressionism is evident also in Spero's *Black Paintings* (1959–64; for example **plates 5–6**), haunting depictions of couples enveloped in nocturnal atmospheres of existential resonance, caught between intense intimacy and impending estrangement. In the

9 Robert Storr, "Peripheral Visions," in the present book, p.27.

late 1960s, the artist abandoned painting on canvas to use paper as support in a series of works that respond with urgency to current political issues: the *War Series* (1966–70; **plates 8–20**), which was prompted by her revolt against the U.S.-led Vietnam War. Inhabited by the touch of Spero's gesture and her selected materials—gouache and ink—the paper surface becomes poetically suggestive of the pliable and sensitive nature of skin. It evokes the fragility of the body as it hosts images of violence, alluding in its sheer materiality to the victims of war—where war is male. Since then, paper—an undervalued medium at the time—became Spero's sounding board, lending an open field for experimentation throughout her practice.[10]

In his 2003 essay "The Weapon and the Wound," first published in the exhibition catalogue *Nancy Spero. The War Series, 1966–1970*, Storr focuses on this body of work and draws a telling parallel between it and Francisco Goya's *Disasters of War* (1810–20; **plate 37**): "Spero's at once harsh and evanescent paintings on paper are stylistically unlike Goya's dense, gritty etchings [...]. Nevertheless, apart from such formal differences these two bodies of work have this in common: both are bitter testaments of disillusionment."[11] The *War Series* were prompted, Storr reminds us, "not only by a general aversion to militarism but also, in quite specific political circumstances, by the sting of promises broken, principles overturned, and the failure of a society to live by its own ideals."[12]

To a work from the *War Series* Spero would turn for inspiration late in life, when she was invited by Storr to make new work for inclusion in the 2007 Venice Biennale exhibition *Think with the Senses / Feel with the Mind*—he was then the Biennale's artistic director. Pushing further

10 In the artist's words: "Abandoning oil painting and switching to paper was a definitive kind of self-realization. Even though I had railed against self-importance, I wanted to expand—I just wanted more space. The confining spaces of small work needed to be augmented—a longer gesture. I had subversive ideas about space in the *War Series* and the *Artaud Paintings*. I wanted to get out in the world and occupy "my" space; it was to become an extended layer of space, primarily horizontal, but also vertical, which could continue virtually indefinitely in extended linear formats." Nancy Spero quoted in "Nancy Spero: The Art of Getting to Equal," *The Feminist Memoir Project: Voices from Women's Liberation*, (Three Rivers Press, New York, 1998), p.366.

11 Robert Storr, "The Weapon and the Wound," in the present book, p.55.

12 Ibid., p.55.

the boundaries of her practice, the artist created her first large-scale sculptural installation, *Maypole / Take No Prisoners* (2007; **plates 73–75**), a compelling site-specific work that inaugurated the exhibition at its Giardini venue, where it occupied the grand entrance hall of the then called Italia Pavilion. As a critic, Storr had written early on, in the late 1980s, on the ability of Spero's art to break down the dichotomy between the analytical and the expressive, the conceptual and the perceptual. In her work, he noted, "each sign, whether graphic or verbal, is both felt and thought."[13] Thereby, her prominent inaugural position in that exhibition was just fitting.

Like many artists do in their late period, and as she had often done through her practice, for her Venice commission Spero revisited an earlier motif and form from her own oeuvre to new ends: she took cues from the 1967 gouache-and-ink-on-paper *Kill Commies / Maypole* (**plate 76**), depicting severed heads dangling from the end of maypole ribbons, with the American flag at the top of the pole. Distilled from that original image, her installation comprises the festive motif of the maypole and the frightening one of the severed head. Hand-printed on aluminum, and double-sided, the screaming heads, many of which with extended tongue—a recurring motif in her oeuvre—hang at head-height, with calibrated variations, from silk ribbons and steel chains attached to a thirty-five-foot aluminum pole positioned at the top of the piece, washed by light from a skylight above it. Hovering just above the viewer, Spero's tormented heads make the encounter with them an intensely emotional confrontation. We are one-on-one with them. They are inescapable. In Venice, with air coming in from the entrance door and visitors moving in space, a light motion invested them, making them gently oscillate, the delicate elegance of that brief motion, almost elegiac, contrasting with the raw brutality of their imagery. When exhibited in 2007 at the Biennale, this work powerfully resonated with the concurrent war in Iraq, as the artist had intended.[14] Exhibited since—notably at The Museum of Modern Art in New York in 2019—it proves to protest the

13 Robert Storr, "Peripheral Visions," in the present book, p.29.

14 In a 2008 interview to *The Brooklyn Rail*, asked about the genesis of the installation, the artist recalled: "When Rob Storr came

brutality of war and violence at large, attesting its ability to continue to echo in unexpected ways with contemporary reality. That is the far-reaching power of Spero's art. It is testified, in particular, by works where the joyful celebration of women emerges increasingly. Consider, for instance, how *Picasso and Frederick's of Hollywood* (1990; **plate 65**)reverberates today in light of the recent international, survivor-led movement (known as MeToo) to end sexual violence and the oppression of women in society. Here, collapsing art history and popular culture, Spero appropriates a Picasso image, a figure culled from the realm of advertising tied to the American lingerie brand Frederick's of Hollywood, and images of ancient goddesses. The figures, that repeat in variations, invoke simultaneously their victimization as objectifications of the male gaze and their liberation from it.[15] That sense of triumph is further articulated through the festive dynamism that imbues much of Spero's production, especially from the 1990s onward, as evidenced, for instance, by works like *The Goddess Nut II*, 1990 (**plate 64**), *Frieze II*, 2001 (**plate 67**), and *Artemis, Acrobats, Divas and Dancers* (2001; **plates 68–72**), the latter a mosaic permanently installed at the 66th Street station of the New York subway at Lincoln Center for the Performing Arts.

Spero's figures dance in space, and it seems that, at any moment, their airy movement could venture out into the space of the viewer. Looking at these images of women today, one finds them contagious in their vitality and their lightness. Gently uplifting, they extend to us an implicit invitation to join them in a movement of liberation. As such, at the current historical juncture, their coming together and their being,

in [sic] his last visit and proposed the front space of one of the pavilions, which was more elevated because of the high ceilings, I thought immediately of [*Kill Commies / Maypole*] being a three-dimensional installation. Similar to the way some have realized how relevant Leon's works were, especially right after the Abu Ghraib episode, I wanted to make a point that there hasn't been that much of a change from what happened in Vietnam and what we're going through right now in Iraq." See "Nancy Spero in Conversation with Phong Bui," *The Brooklyn Rail* (July–August 2008): https://brooklynrail.org/2008/07/art/nancy-spero-in-conversation-with-phong-bui/.

The reference is to the Iraq War which began in 2003, launched by U.S.-led invasion, and ended in 2011.

15 The image of the Picasso's woman comes from his 1937 painting *La Baignade* (On the Beach), in the Peggy Guggenheim Collection, Venice.

at the same time, one and plural celebrate open-endedness and complexity in ways that make them indispensable.

Spero's women continue to inspire the breaking down of hierarchies and the engagement in a resilient battle to expand the possibilities of woman in society. The dialogical dimension they give life to is an antidote to the rigid, one-dimensional approach erasing differences and contradiction that too often prevails in contemporary culture.

Their call for revolt against the injustice perpetrated on the vulnerable has the power to expand across gender, ethnicity, and culture, and radiates today with timely urgency. For Spero's women seem to dance to an unrelentless song of great resonance:

You may shoot me with your words,
You may cut me with your eyes,
You may kill me with your hatefulness,
But still, like air, I'll rise.[16]

16 The quote is from Maya Angelou's poem *Still I Rise* (1978), which has also inspired the title of the present essay.

Notes on Nancy

by Robert Storr

The art world—composed in varying proportions of commerce and seat-of-the-pants journalism too often confused with scholarship—generally gives short shrift to artists who refuse to fit into existing art critical/art historical categories. But the misfits are frequently the most interesting and most substantial exponents of the new, although they are just as frequently taxed or bypassed for being too early or too late to represent the trends to which they gave primary, if not definitive, expression.

Such has been the case with the American artist Nancy Spero (1926–2009). Her roots being in the Midwest, a degree of regional marginalization always threatened her reputation, despite the transhistorical and fundamentally cosmopolitan frames of reference of her art—especially so in the largely New York-centered art world of the 1970s and 1980s when she fully emerged. Most importantly, Spero eschewed most of the "mainstream" esthetic discourses of her day starting with New York School Abstract Expressionism on down through Pop art and Minimalism—although she knew closely Pop practitioner Claes Oldenburg who, like her, studied at the School of the Art Institute of Chicago (SAIC), and she shared political convictions with him during the 1970s and 1980s, and, furthermore, in the mid-1970s she made common cause with Minimalist artist Carl Andre in activist matters.

The American art writer Christopher Lyon has authored the best, most comprehensive monograph to date about the artist's oeuvre, and a spate of exhibition catalogues attest to the high esteem in which she is held among scholars, critics, and members of the dedicated art public.[1]

In particular, she was the subject of a major survey at the Everson Museum of Art in Syracuse, New York in 1987, *Nancy Spero: Works Since 1950*, organized by Dominique Nahas. (One of the essays featured in this volume was originally my contribution to the catalogue of that show.)[2] That survey traveled to multiple venues in the United States

1 Christopher Lyon, *Nancy Spero: The Work* (Prestel, Munich and New York, 2010).

2 Robert Storr, "Nancy Spero: Central Issues – Peripheral Visions" in the present book, pp.33–46.

and Canada, including New York's New Museum, located at the time at 583 Broadway. Since the Syracuse exhibition, Spero has had a fairly steady stream of one-person exhibitions attesting to her importance as a contemporary artist on both sides of the Atlantic. Notably, these have included retrospectives at the Reina Sofia in Madrid (2008), the Centre Georges Pompidou in Paris (2010), and the Serpentine Gallery in London (2011). Furthermore, a major overview of her oeuvre, *Nancy Spero: Paper Mirror*, was presented at New York's MoMA PS1 (2019) by Peter Eleey—the exhibition was originally organized for the Museo Rufino Tamayo in Mexico City in 2018 by Julie Ault (**plate 77**).[3] In particular, in the MoMA PS1 show Spero's seminal multi-panel installation *Notes in Time* (1976–79), from the museum's own collection, was prominently displayed in its sprawling entirety. As these key elements of her exhibition history point out, Spero is hardly an art world underdog. And yet, the full measure of her richly complex contribution, and the degree to which it continues to defy existing art critical/art historical categories, has yet to be taken.

In all the literature devoted to Spero her fervent feminism is cited, almost to the exclusion of other qualities. But she was many things aside from her consistent emphasis on gender issues—which prompted her total exclusion of representations of men from her work since 1976, though she often cited male thinkers and writers in the texts she incorporated in her reference-rich collages. The practice of assimilating what men had said about women over the course of history into wide amalgams of pictures and graphic activity made her a bellwether for the art of appropriation in general, *avant la lettre*, but it also provided a critical context against which she and the viewer could push. Her work achieves that primarily by making explicit ancient misogynistic prejudices which, for the most part, go unspoken and acquire much of their subtle as well as blunt force power by passing for common sense. So doing, Spero launched these emblems of bigotry into play like the ball in roulette, spinning round and round until finally settling into place with jarring

3 Editor's note: The exhibition *Nancy Spero: Paper Mirror* was held at Museo Tamayo, Mexico City, (6 October 2018 – 17 February 2019) and subsequently took place at MoMA PS1, New York (31 March – 23 June 2019).

effect in proximity to a space reserved for representations and citations of generally accepted "truisms" about the "inherent" nature of men and women and their "innate differences."

For the rest, many of the most provocatively gendering statements to which the artist makes recourse are culled from the writings of Hélène Cixous, Luce Irigaray, and other third-wave French feminists who emerged as fundamental figures in the cultural debate in the mid-1990s. Originally, the first wave of the feminist movement (spanning from the mid-19th century to 1920) had been prompted by the British and American Suffragettes' struggle for the vote and legal parity, and the second wave (from the 1960s to the early 1980s), of which Spero was actively part, had been set in motion by a widespread delving into and defiance of ideological constraints on women, constraints keyed to sociological, psychological, and philosophical assumptions and considerations which Simone de Beauvoir had effectively summarized and disputed in her seminal 1949 book *Le Deuxième Sexe* (The Second Sex). Born in Cleveland, Ohio in 1926, and grown up in Chicago, where in 1949 she graduated from SAIC, Spero, together with her husband, the American artist Leon Golub (1922–2004), whom she married in 1951, lived in Paris from 1959 to 1964, where she created her first mature works, the *Black Paintings*. Spero ended up in the right place at the right time: in Paris she immersed herself in and absorbed these influential, feminist-oriented currents of critical discourse. In 1964 she settled in New York, where she lived and worked ever since.

Missing from this summary, so far, are some crucial existential contingencies including the fact that during the course of these transitional years she became the mother of three boys and was generally best known in the art world as *the wife of* the contrarian painter Golub, who was famously out of step with the New York School "mainstream." Nevertheless, from the time of their meeting as students at SAIC in 1946, Spero and Golub conducted their creative and social lives as a team, although one composed of autonomous individuals with shared convictions and esthetic predispositions. Even to the point of dividing down the middle their loft on LaGuardia Place in New York, just above Soho, where they settled in 1972 and spent the second, most productive half of their creative lives. Nancy had a bedroom in the back of one half of the loft, Leon his own quarters in the other. All the rest of the space was devoted to making and storing their respective work, with a kitchen in between where they received guests and held meetings of the many, diverse political coalitions in which they participated.

Mostly, their social circle was made up of sympathetic writers, artists, and curators. In the first group, they ranged from hipster Peter Schjeldahl, who briefly flirted with Golub's work as an extension of his attraction to edgy, male-centered painterly or Neo-Expressionist painting, to Jo Anna Isaak, who championed Spero's feminism in the presence of which Schjeldahl cowered. Also of note in this group was the acerbic art historian/critic Robert Pincus-Witten, a "red diaper" baby turned waspish esthete who had known Spero and Golub since their Chicago days and who attended many of their at-home gatherings—incidentally, he used to remember being served what he called, referencing the Mexican staple, "refried beans." In addition, the couple's milieu encompassed fellow artists and activists ranging from Anna Mendieta and Carl Andre to Claes Oldenburg and Coosje van Bruggen, to David Wojnarowicz and fellow SAIC grad of the 1950s and lifelong Leftist, painter, and master of pastel, as well as Paris-based ex-pat, Irving Petlin. Spero and Golub entered into all of these communities and into activist organizations jointly—except for New York's A.I.R. (Artists in Residence) Gallery, a woman's cooperative of which, since 1972, Nancy was an original member, together with Barbara Zucker, Judith Bernstein, and Dotty Attie. When in the 1980s Nancy was given an opportunity to make a work on the electric billboards in New York's Times Square, Leon, ever her loyal male feminist consort, suggested that, in fairness, he deserved to have one too, and jokingly added that his would flash, "Nancy, what's for dinner?"[4] As

4 Editor's note: In 1986, Spero was invited to participate in the program "Messages to the Public" where artists received a 30-second time slot for a video artwork after each 30 minutes of advertising on the Spectacolor advertising board at New York's One Times Square. (The program ran from 1982 to 1990 and included artists such as Keith Haring and Barbara Kruger, to name a few.) For it, Spero made a piece consisting in a feminist and pro-choice message comprising an Aztec quote and a statement by her. It was never played publicly—Spectacolor canceled it due to its content. The work was shown only once to be photographed for documentation by the Public Art Fund.

a rule, though, the couple ate in neighborhood restaurants or ordered take-out for however many people happened to be around the studio when meal time arrived. Theirs was a Spartan, no-nonsense version of the Art World Merry Go Round of the era, more a make-do-with-what-you-have 1960s and 1970s style life than a go-for-broke 1980s performance of high bohemian style. As a successful art couple, Leon and Nancy were well known in Chicago when I attended SAIC in the late 1970s, and their door in New York was open throughout the 1980s to anyone with a serious interest in their work and the causes they explored politically. Moreover, Leon hired me to fill in for him at Rutgers, The State University of New Jersey, in New Brunswick when he needed to take a break from teaching, and together he and Nancy recommended me as artist for shows in New York in the 1980s at The Judson Memorial Church (such shows focused on opposition to the U.S. intervention in Central America during the Reagan administration) and at The Lesbian and Gay Community Services Center (today The Lesbian, Gay, Bisexual & Transgender Community Center) where I participated in *The Center Show* (1989).[5]

Spero's work while in Paris consisted of figurative paintings of men and women engulfed in ominous black atmospheres (**plates 5–6**). The drawing in them probes that darkness, but never fully fathoms it, implying that it was an all consuming, all obscuring state of being. When Spero returned to the United States in 1964, the War in Vietnam was ramping up (it would last from 1955 to 1975). That civil war between the North and the South was a continuation of the anti-colonial struggle against the French government, a struggle parallel to that of the Algerians for the independence from France (fought from 1954 to 1962), which Spero and Golub had experienced and felt keenly during their expatriate life in Paris. Accordingly, Spero started to translate press pictures of the fighting and the hardware deployed in Vietnam—machine guns, choppers and bombs—into deft gestural images on canvas and paper, contrasting the delicacy of her marks and the

5 Editor's note: *The Center Show* was organized by curators Rick Barnett and Barbara Sahlman. Participating artists included Jane Dickson, General Idea, Leon Golub, Guerilla Girls, David LaChapelle, Barbara Sandler, Nancy Spero, and Robert Storr, among others.

support on which she made them—she worked increasingly on paper to the eventual exclusion of canvas (**plates 8–18, 20**). This juxtaposition of heavily worked forms and fragile grounds, of hands-off, photomechanical imagery with spontaneously emotive mark-making effectively conflated the two contending esthetics that were to dominate the 1980s, but without resulting in a stable synthesis. Each piece evoked unresolved, perhaps unresolvable, contradictions but provided proof of what was at stake—that is to say, what was gained and what was lost if one chose one side of the dispute over the other logically rather than intuitively based on the immediate options made available by praxis. Thus, in subsequent years Spero's work was a critical battleground between the two main avant-garde schools of thought, namely Neo-Expressionism and text and photo-based appropriation art. The *War Paintings*, or *War Series*, occupied the artist from 1966 to 1970, at which juncture she shifted gear to confront violence allegorically in the *Codex Artaud* (1971–72; **plates 28–29, 30–31, 32, 33, 34**)—her pivotal work in the development of her singular practice. To that purpose, she ventriloquized her own female anguish through the borrowed male voice of the accursed, misogynist French poet and playwright Antonin Artaud. This wrenching gender reversal was a bold move that by-passed academic thinking and freed Spero emotionally and formally. Thereafter, starting in 1976, she resolved to deploy only female protagonists, and concentrated on the making and layout of paper scrolls of the kind used in the *Codex Artaud*.

Thus, for the next 39 of her 83 years, Spero tilled the ground she had opened up in the *Codex*, mapping its full thematic extent and cultivating the unexpected graphic and syntactic *trouvailles* of her exploratory working process. First and foremost, she pressed outward on the format itself. Finding inspiration, among other sources, in the tradition of ancient friezes as well as of European art scrolls, which had been an eloquent vehicle for story telling since the Bayeux Tapestry, Spero deployed the linear design of the paper to propel the chronicles she was recording in vivid pictorial episodes, which in the main constituted the unwritten *her*story of women in Western history. Its chapters leap-frogged between remote but exultant past—for example, represented by dancing Greek figures or grotesque carvings of Sheela na Gig (a primitive female spirit out of Celtic folk legends)—and lacerating contemporary events—such as the then interminable Vietnam war (**plates 8–18, 20**) and the persecution of Leftists in Chile after the Pinochet coup (**plate 36**).[6]

Overtly didactic, Spero did not shy away from explicit content of any kind. History painters, of which she was uniquely one, never have. By the same token, though, her collage approach of patching together words and images from multiple sources meant that her scrolls were intrinsically dialectic as well, speaking with many voices rather than just one. Thus, she ceded authorial power to a plurality of personae rather than proposing or pretending to represent just one version of femininity in an ideal, essentialized form, juxtaposing as she did contrasting perspectives and tonal registers of a chorus of women across time. To that end, she included some male declarations as well. For example, in her *Notes in Time*, that of fashionable French critical theorist, Jacques Derrida (**plate 47**), who served as a paradoxically chauvinist foil for enlightened feminism, demonstrating that one could be at the cutting edge of the "new" in one domain and woefully *reactionary* in an adjacent one. This put Spero in the front lines of those who resisted the dubious, usually masculine bullying inherent in so much postmodern discourse. Furthermore, overall, her work's facture disputed by example many of the received ideas that drove North American "theory heads" to dogmatic extremes at the end of the twentieth century based on their tendentious misreading of Walter Benjamin's pivotal postmodernist essay *The Work of Art in the Age of Mechanical Reproduction* (1935). Instead of illustrating theoretical positions once they had been arrived at rationally, Spero preferred to make use of everything within her reach eliminating theoretical positions only when they failed the empirical test of fully embodying her dilemmas, even as she insisted that those dilemmas be felt as well.

6 Ironically enough, Pinochet seized power on 9/11/73 meaning that simply citing "9/11" as a day that shall live in infamy can boomerang on chauvinistic Americans considering our government's indisputable hand in giving the Right wing generals in Chile the edge in their efforts to topple the duly elected President Salvador Allende.

Spero's installation for the Venice Biennale of 2007, titled *Maypole / Take No Prisoners* (**plates 73–75**), brought all of these concerns into play. It was her last major piece. Commissioned for the main hub of the Venice Biennale's international group exhibition *Think with the Senses / Feel with the Mind* (2007) presented in the former Italian Pavillon in the Giardini and organized by the author of this monograph and his curatorial colleague, Francesca Pietropaolo (who is also the editor of this small monograph and the series to which it belongs), Spero's work consisted of flat aluminum profiles cut out and silkscreened with drawings of women's heads shouting or screaming while encircling a central shaft to which they were attached by colorful ribbons that, in their carnivalesque gaiety, were cognitively dissonant with the expressions on the faces of those who synesthetically made up this polyphonic chorus of anguish and rage. Call them harpies if you must, theirs was a raucous yet righteous rejoinder to the normalizing art world jabber about "political" art of academically sanctioned varieties. And, as such, an Artaudesque shriek of anger and pain in which anyone and everyone so inclined could join. When the chronicle of postwar, postmodern women's art is written, it should henceforth be centered on Spero as much as anyone, for *her*story was a long, polysemic saga.

Peripheral Visions

First published in Parkett
(December 1987), no.14, pp.6–10.

Increasingly, postmodernism in New York has become the affair of fainthearted suicides. Perched on every available ledge in a city of skyscrapers—to the ablest climbers go the most visible—they proclaim the nullity of contemporary life and the end of art. Yet, somehow these avatars of ennui just can't bring themselves to take the definitive step. And while they contemplate the abyss in a state of dramatized inertia, we watch them from below with rapt indifference. This reciprocal fixation is called "closure." No one, it seems, has sufficient sense, or pity, to yell, "Jump!"

Yet, it is action we crave, and a release from numbed voyeurism. And, outside the closed circle of this static spectacle, things are moving. Regardless of the prevailing assumption that our "fin de siècle" is an epoch of ceaseless repetition, there are growing signs of change. Not for the better, in all likelihood, but change nonetheless. For few at the top or bottom of society have the luxury of standing still. A senescent president muffs his lines but delegates his powers to mercenaries. Anticolonial wars of liberation become national wars of attrition, which the "Big Powers" seek to manage. The combatants, however, remain murderously unmanageable. Meanwhile, with economic "booms" having a proven tendency to convert themselves into "busts," the speculative euphoria of the early 1980s dissipates. Already, giddiness has set in. Soon, more resolute sky-divers may be crowding access to the highest windows.

Despite ourselves, we are about to be thrust back into "history." The question is what—if any—art can respond to the dislocations that are destined, and what art is ample or savvy enough to convincingly instruct those who mistook sloganeering and publicity for analysis, and TV time for their own uncertain lifespan. Not many come to mind. Of those who do, curiously enough, there are several already relegated to the purgatory of the immediate past. Chief among them is the painter-collagist Nancy Spero. Known as a "feminist"—which she most certainly is, but which label has become a primary means of isolating and so disregarding her achievement—Spero, now in her sixties, is notable for her stamina and her stubborn refusal to be boxed in by stylistic, ideological, or generational labels. All these factors would seem to suggest an eccentric, perhaps intractable art. Instead, Spero's work distinguishes itself by its openness and dynamism. That dynamism is of a unique variety.

Choosing her subject matter from the writings of French poet and playwright Antonin Artaud (**plates 22–27**)—a genuine modernist who, to use his words, was all but "suicided by society"—from grisly press reports of the persecution of political activists in the Third World (**plate 36**), and from the mythic conflicts of the Gods, Spero strews her tableaux with episodes of extreme violence and anguish. Often, and most especially in her work of the 1970s, these images are rendered in a graphic manner of incomparable emotional urgency. Her gesture is sharp and concise, her surfaces sore with abrasions, her colors a peculiar range of bruised ochres and black. For all that, however, her pictures do not preach to us from the position of a secure and earnest "humanism"—to choose the malignant and often misogynistic writings of Artaud as her text raises many of the same issues and ambivalences as Simone de Beauvoir's perversely pioneering feminist essay, "Must We Burn Sade?"[1] Much less, for all its expressivity, is Spero's work, in the conventional sense of the term, "Neo-Expressionist."

Quite the opposite. Much of the new Expressionist work either implicitly or explicitly reinvokes the romantic cult of the painter as hero living out freedoms lesser men and women have been obliged to forswear. The subject of these paintings are the acts of individuals, their scale a metaphor for the grandiosity of the artist's vision, their heft and "value" a promise of permanence. Everything in Spero's work contradicts these expectations. Spero has rendered the fat of Expressionism and preserved the sinew and the skin. Thus, though vigorous figures animate her work, and touch informs it, Spero's paintings, drawings, and collages are remarkable for their almost ephemeral physical presence. Cut like monstrous paper-dolls or stamped with brittle contours on otherwise denuded sheets of paper joined end to end in scrolls, the very delicacy of her often tiny images heightens our

1 Editor's note: Simone de Beauvoir, "Faut-il brûler Sade ?" originally published in *Les temps modernes* (December 1951), no.74, pp.1002–1033 and *Les temps modernes* (January 1952), no.75, pp.1197–1230. First translated into English as "Must We Burn Sade?" by Annette Michelson in *The Marquis de Sade* (Grove Press, New York, 1966).

awareness of the extreme situations to which they allude. And while heroes—or rather heroines—do appear from time to time, never does their maker intrude as a principal protagonist. What enthralls us is not the drama of the artistic creation but the political, historical, and sexual dramas to which Spero, like us, is witness.

It is a drama of carnal torment, rebellion, and celebration. In it, women struggle against the violence done to them, parade their vitality, and mock the authorities that would confine them to their rhetorical "place." In *Notes in Time* (begun in 1976 and completed in 1979), for example, a nude female figure, legs spread, is catapulted over the quotation from Jacques Derrida: "there is no essence of woman ... there is no truth about woman ... the feminist women ... are men" (**plate 47**). Such critical counterpoint between text and image is essential to Spero's enterprise, and, it should be added, it has been characteristic of her work since long before the advent of currently fashionable forms of appropriation and deconstruction. The constant slippage from one representational code (pictures) to another (words), and often their jarring confrontation, results in a fully realized dialectic between perceptual apprehension and conceptual inquiry. Images do not exist merely as talking heads for a more important critical soundtrack, nor do words merely caption visual scenarios. Each sign, whether graphic or verbal, is both felt and thought. Each discourse is interrupted and answered by its contrary. Tidiness is inimical to her purpose.

To accommodate such a multiplicity of voices and languages, Spero has improvised a new pictorial format. Stretching the standard rectangle into long ribbons over which are distributed a wealth of disparate incidents, Spero has arrived at the perfect structure for a discursive as opposed to a narrative art, an unframed, uncompartmentalized version of the "bande dessinée." (The English term comic strip emphasizes content over form and is, for that reason, less useful here.) Hung in disjunctive groupings, some of these segments are positioned vertically and others horizontally. As in the case of the *Codex Artaud* (1971–72; **plates 28–29, 30–31, 32, 33, 34**), the measurements of each distinct section may run from twenty inches in width to sixteen to thirty feet in length or height. On several occasions, moreover, Spero has overstepped the edge of her paper support and printed images directly on the wall, in a Lascaux-like dispersion of phantom silhouettes. What Spero has done is to explode the conventional pictorial grid and permit its axes to extend at will in all directions. To follow the complex detail and grasp the complex syntax of a given series of these pictorial fragments one must constantly readjust one's gaze, jumping from one extreme of vision to another and then back to images too hastily scanned in the process.

In this respect, "reading" a work by Spero is akin to reading stanzas of shaped verse projected on a mural scale. And as with the best of concrete poetry, one experiences a uniquely active visual and intellectual engagement. Contradictions, digressions, and ruptures in the flow of the line do not engender the sense of confusion and stasis that is evident in much recent work using the closed framing of the traditional easel painting as a means to impose an absolute relativism on a host of incommensurable symbols and modes of address. Rather, the notion of dynamic simultaneity, which was the hallmark of early modernism, returns within a new and expansive structure. The key lies with the viewer's capacity to exploit peripheral vision as a way of encompassing a whole that is always about to exceed one's scope, while at the same time using focused vision as a way to take full account of each of the dense images and phrases that flash within that field.

This, then, is the formal structure of a new "history painting." For that is what Spero has been up to for the past twenty years. Cross-referencing icons from the past with documents and emblems that invoke current events, her codices—contemporary hieroglyphic chronicles—depict a synchronous and thoroughly modern sense of time. No "mainstream" obtains; the sequencing of images is dispersed and channeled by numerous currents, tributaries, and deltas. None of the "great narratives" circumscribes the range of her interests—neither that of Sigmund Freud, nor Karl Marx, nor any of the more recent theorists—yet all find a place within the spacious framework of her work, which also incorporates the generally ignored stories of the sexual, cultural, and economic "Other." Nor is any apocalypse foreseen, nor any halt to the challenges of perpetual flux. To grasp meaning thus requires a temporal equivalent to peripheral vision, a full acknowledgement of our involuntary and discomforting capacity for simultaneously looking back and thinking forward. "History is a nightmare from which I am trying to awake," wrote James Joyce at the beginning of the modernist age.[2] Perhaps the most radical and truthful admission at the end of the modern epoch is that there is no "end," and that we have been awake all along. The idea of finality, it turns out, has been a weary daydream. Hence, in the last analysis, postmodernism demonstrates that we cannot outrun, reenact, or stop history—though we may at any point put a stop to ourselves—but must live in it as fully conscious of our circumstances as curiosity and tolerance will allow. Spero is one of a small contingent of artists who make that alternative seem not only conceivable, but, in brief moments, hopeful.

2 Editor's note: James Joyce, *Ulysses* (Shakespeare and Company, Paris, 1922), p.34.

Nancy Spero: Central Issues – Peripheral Visions

First published in Leon Golub, Jo-Anna Isaak, Ronald A. Kuchta, Dominique Nahas, and Robert Storr, Nancy Spero. Works Since 1950, *exh. cat. (Everson Museum of Art, Syracuse, N.Y., 1987), pp.44–62.*

An artist is measured, in the first instance, by the difficulty of the problems she chooses to confront. For the past twenty years, Nancy Spero has addressed the most vexing of all: those which condition our expectations of and response to socially engaged art. The very intractability of those expectations, and the frequent confusion of "art world" politics—that is to say, the stylistic novelty and attendant philosophical fads—with politics in the larger sense have tended to obscure Spero's long-term project. At the same time, however, the critical and imaginative sterility they have engendered—not to mention the cynicism—now highlights her achievement. Stamina and an inherent disinclination to supply tidy answers to complex issues have been the keys to her survival. The key to her achievement is Spero's persistent efforts to synthesize private experience and public memory. In a period of ideological contraction, this tendency to insist upon the equality of and fertile relation between the two halves of this equation is a considerable inconvenience to some. Even more inconvenient is Spero's habit of picturing the plurality of forms they may take. Rather than merely phrasing the question of "difference," she has sought to catalogue "otherness" in all its sexual, historical, cultural, and expressive variety. Yet contesting the conventional wisdom of the moment is always the first task of the radical. Spero has been about it a long while, but never has her contribution been more timely or more resonant.

The traditional imperative of political art is to "say" something. Outrage, hope, solidarity—these emotions demand expression, and the presumed audience, varied and easily distracted as it is, would seem to require that what is said is said without equivocation. Thus, "sincerity" disallows ambiguity or ambivalence, urgency prohibits complexity. So goes the logic and therein lies its flaw. For, in relying upon uniform strategies within which only the signs are changed, all such propagandistic art looks fundamentally the same. Meaning for the public is reduced to reflex identification—"Which side are you on?"—while the essential structures of thought remain intact. At the same time, the committed artist is reduced to a mere technician—"You don't need a weather man to know which way the wind blows"—obliged to emblazon certainties that they themselves do not possess. Indeed, to succeed at this task is possible only at the cost of ceasing to be political, that is to say, actively engaged in a radical re-examination of prevailing social constructs.

Habits such as these are hard, if not impossible, to break in the heat of action. Thus, though the 1960s was an era of profound dislocation and protracted struggle, little of the art prompted by the civil rights and anti-Vietnam War movements was either of esthetic or intellectual consequence. Of the few notable exceptions, two in particular stick in mind. And they do so insofar as they seem in retrospect to adumbrate the art of the 1980s. Thus, the gallows humor of Barnett Newman's *Lace Curtain for Mayor Daley* (1968) transcends its topical pretext. Combining symbolic literalism (barbed wire) with sculptural literalism (the steel rectangle and grid), Newman's piece looks forward to Hans Haacke's grim parody of the Minimalist cube, *U.S. Isolation Box, Grenada 1983* (1984). In a similar fashion, but with far more wrenching effect, the poster of the My Lai massacre published by Art Workers Coalition in 1969 looked forward to deconstructive appropriation. Showing the bloodied victims in a ditch over which were printed the simple question asked Lieutenant Calley during his trial, "And Babies?" and Calley's affirmation "And Babies," the war came home as never before.

Contrary to expectations, the awful eloquence of this poster was a consequence of its editorial reticence. Turned against itself, the "objectivity" of media was used to probe the subjectivity of the viewer on the one hand, and the hidden agenda of power on the other. Variants on these two means of ideological "sabotage," the intransigent object and the trenchant but disembodied text, have informed most advanced political art since that time. The snarling villains and virile heroes of the past have faded into echo-chambered voices and photographic specters. So much so that it is now widely assumed that political art is by definition impersonal in its facture and indirect in its address. So much so indeed that the hand-made work—with painting and drawing its most prized manifestations—is understood to be by definition a conservative if not avowedly retrograde form. Thus, Formalism in its Minimalist and Conceptualist permutations has been reconnected to politics—long ago sacrificed by Clement Greenberg to the demands of pure delectation—constituting a new

Left "mainstream," the antithesis of which is commonly thought to be the "Neo-Expressionism" of recent years.

Missing from this equation, however, is consideration of the work of a handful of veteran "Expressionist" painters who made dramatic changes in their work in the mid-1960s in direct response to the upheavals of the time. Between 1966 and 1968, Philip Guston, for one, abandoned gestural abstraction for figurative scenarios replete with the political symbols of his youth. With this distinction: rather than pointing his finger at his brutish Ku Klux Klansmen as if they were a remote or alien nemesis, Guston, draping the artist in a hood as well, was pointing it at himself. America had met the enemy and it was us. Nor was Guston alone, as Harold Rosenberg said, in having "risked a fully developed career on the possibility of engaging art in the political reality."[1] At much the same time, Leon Golub left behind the mythic iconography of his *Gigantomachies*, and embarked on work which involved the direct but increasingly ambiguous quotation of news photographs of world leaders and their minions. Thus, contrary to the now conventional wisdom, some of the boldest and most complex radical art of the period was the product of artists steeped in the tradition of painting. As a consequence, they were acutely aware of the possibilities as well as the abused prerogatives of painting.

Missing also from the equation is the contribution of the "first" generation of feminist artists. For, more than any movement, it was feminism, in all its various aspects, that provided the forum for a continued debate over the means and ends of political art in the aftermath of the 1960s. In fact, feminism flourished in the ruins of the anti-war movement and the breakup of the civil rights coalition. In part a rebuke to the factionalism and chauvinism that, by shutting down argument, had contributed so much to their demise, feminism was the pre-eminent expression of the social and esthetic pluralism of the 1970s. Breaking into the art world for the first time, women brought with them the full range of ideas and methods they had developed during the long years they had been restricted to its margins. Their entry thus

1 Harold Rosenberg, "Liberation from Detachment," in *The De-Definition of Art* (Horizon Press, New York, 1972), p.140.

constituted a major challenge to the orthodoxies that had held sway over the previous two generations, and a temporary hiatus in, if not the beginning of the end of, New York hegemony.

Most closely associated with the latter group, Nancy Spero rightfully belongs to the first as well. But her membership, like that of Frida Kahlo among the Mexican muralists, is an exceptional and a dissenting one. For not only has Spero worked against the current of Formalist abstraction, Pop art, and other critically sanctioned styles, for all the emotional power of her work, she has also from the very first worked separately from the dominant tendencies of postwar painterly figuration. Fiercely independent of the New York School, and, despite her five-year sojourn in Paris, equally so of its European sources and imitators, Spero, like her Chicago colleagues, took her cue from the ethnographic objects they discovered at the Field Museum [of Natural History, Chicago]—witness her early fetish-like head *Mummified* (c.1950–51)—and the *Art Brut* championed by Jean Dubuffet, the most influential outsider to visit Chicago during Spero's years at the School of the Art Institute in the late 1950s. At the same time, however, though Spero shared these enthusiasms with other members of her generation, her first mature work has none of the overtly grotesque, much less funky, aspect to that of her peers. Less essays in generalized essential anguish than lyric, albeit bleak, studies of the estrangement and mutual dependence of couples, Spero's *Black Paintings* of the early 1960s are remarkable for their very lack of rhetorical violence or painterly flourish (**plates 5–6**). Their plainness is their truth. In a period rife with images of gorgons and "cuties," their subtle female eroticism made them virtually unique.

As singular and as evocative as these paintings remain, however, Spero's real break-through did not come until the mid-1960s. Public events, combined with an uneasiness about the slow, groping process this work entailed, precipitated the change. Returning to the United States in 1964, Spero ran headfirst into the prevailing taste for "cool" art, and, for the first time, confronted the "hot" war in Vietnam in daily television installments. The first heightened her resolve to make the most of her "outsider" status. Paris and Chicago, with their relative tolerance for aggressive art, had provided a safe haven; New York forced a more determined resistance to fashion and to impotent isolation. The second factor, Vietnam, caused her to abandon the amorphous figures and ambiguous situations she had concentrated on in favor of stark statements about the death and destruction wreaked by the American war machine. Yet, for all their topicality—Spero calls them "broadsides"—the *War Series* (1966–70; **plates 8–18, 20**) nonetheless depicted the conflict in almost archetypal terms while affording her the opportunity to experiment with the basic formal elements she would employ for the next twenty years. Thus, her renderings of insect-like or reptilian aircraft in metallic paints enhance an already horrifying iconic presence with an apt and chilling use of contemporary materials. Loosely but exactingly delineated on rice paper, these drawings combine an extreme delicacy of facture with an extraordinary pictorial ferocity. In this regard, they are reminiscent of those produced by survivors of Hiroshima and Nagasaki. Finally, in these works Spero for the first time began to incorporate words—or more accurately, to abrasively juxtapose words with the image. Thus, Pentagon double-speak—*pacification, search and destroy*—are set against the devastation Pentagon policy brought about.

Yet, it would have been impossible to foresee in the relative self-containment and sincere humanism of these works the expansiveness and the bitterness of those which came next. Introduced by one of her sons to the writing of Antonin Artaud, the extremity of the seer-pamphleteer's alienation struck a deep chord in Spero.[2] In some respects, this affinity for Artaud might seem problematic. Many artists succumbing to self-pity have felt, as Artaud claimed, "suicided by society." The denial of such obsessive self-absorption was one of the implicit goals of 1960s art and, more particularly, the explicit subject of Allan Kaprow's astringent but cleansing essay *The Artist as Man of the World* (1964). On other levels, Spero's interest in Artaud might appear positively perverse. Though this was prior to her active involvement in feminist causes, Artaud's misogyny was hard to miss, as was his pathological and latently fascist enthusiasm for convulsive ritual.

2 Antonin Artaud (1896–1948), French poet, playwright, stage and film actor, director, and visual artist.

But if Artaud considered himself a victim of society, more fundamental was his obsession with the duality of mind and body and his agonizing sensitivity to the treachery of language. Deconstructionist *avant la lettre*, Artaud understood the manner in which the word reveals and enforces the will of power while rendering certain ideas unthinkable because unsayable. The task of the poet, as he described it in the fragmentary, polyvocal, and incantatory nature of his writing, was to open and extend language beyond its "logical" syntactic limits and, at least momentarily, to give full utterance a pure anarchic being. "A man possesses himself in flashes," he wrote Jacques Rivière, "and even when he possesses himself he does not reach himself completely. He does not realize that constant cohesion of his forces without which all true creation is impossible. Nevertheless, this man exists."[3] Such intermittent clarity is the best we can hope for. Yet, we long for an integration of experience our mind can conceive but not achieve. That is the anxious dialectic we must endure.

It is to these sentiments that Spero responded most immediately, and these perspectives that the world itself ultimately accords. What was required was a new graphic language. Artistic invention, however, is never dictated by "objective" esthetic need alone. And, if an artist succeeds in establishing a genuine congruence between one medium and another or their work and that of another, it is out of parallel intuition, not just a consciously shared formal intention. To that extent, Spero's works are not adaptations or embellishments of Artaud's text so much as the reenactment in pictorial terms of his dilemma. It was her own personal requirements and circumstances, not his, that were at issue.

In setting aside the conventions, materials, and formats of oil painting, Spero had also called into question ideas about the relation of process to product that had to a large measure dictated the emotional impact of her work. Whereas in her *Black Paintings*, the images struggled to emerge from and then appeared to sink back into the primal

3 Antonin Artaud, *Selected Writings of Artaud*, Susan Sontag ed., Helen Weaver trans. (Farar, Straus and Giroux, New York, 1976), p.43.

murk of the ground, in subsequent work on paper Spero placed them on empty white fields, forcing her to confront the full reality and intensity of her emotions as never before. Recalling the radicalization she was undergoing as "a very private thing," the shift in emphasis from the *War Series* to the *Artaud Paintings* (1969–70; **plates 22–27**) and eventually to the *Codex Artaud* (1971–72; **plates 28–29, 30–31, 32, 33, 34**) represents a jump from focused social outrage to rage pure and simple; a deep and pervasive malaise as unexpected and at least as disquieting to her as to the viewer. Here "practical" considerations entered in a uniquely far-reaching way. Working at home and concerned lest these images and the feelings they bespoke upset her children, Spero dramatically modified her technique. Making tiny drawings in the relative privacy of the tabletop, Spero would cover them with any words whatsoever. *The First Language* (1981; **plates 55–56**) is almost pure pleasure; a visually lean and deftly choreographed chorus of gestures, all of which announce a newfound confidence and psychic freedom.

To the degree such work represents women as a "natural" force unleashed against the fortress of male "culture," or re-presents positive archetypes of women as glimpsed in modern heroines or myriad incarnations of ancient goddesses, one might well see it as belonging to the feminism of the 1970s. Indeed, Spero's work does, in fact, constitute one of the definitive statements of that project and period. Yet, to limit one's estimation of its ambition and significance to strictly iconographic issues is to miss the point. Though Spero deliberately describes the world from a female perspective, her preoccupations exceed any narrowly conceived political agenda, and certainly they transcend the "gender-cult" tendencies of the previous decade. Rather, the essential content and radical contribution of her work are most concretely stated by its formal conception, scope, and rigor.

As should be obvious, Spero has stood apart from artistic fashion throughout her career. Still, what is most striking in the last analysis is not the conventions and clichés she has disdained, so much as the contradictions she has embraced. It is the specific nature of these contradictions and the synthesis she has effected that make her work utterly contemporary, and an essential contribution to the deadlocked debate over the relative advantages and ideological entanglements of the hand-made object and the machine-produced multiple. For insofar as Spero has joined in criticizing the "machismo" of much recent painterly figuration, made use of appropriation, and explored the dialectic of textual and pictorial representation, she has done so without falling prey to a simple—much less simple-minded—dichotomization of the expressive touch and repetitive imprint, the singular and the generic image. Rather, Spero puts maximum pressure on the visual and theoretical tension between the two extremes. Alert to the potency of recognition and reiteration in her use of borrowed forms, Spero has remained just as conscious of the discursive possibilities of drawing and its graphic analogues. In the scuffed, silhouetted figures of the 1970s, for example, the artist created a race of monsters that recall those of the past, yet are new.[4] Thus, a dragon that appears in *Torture of Women* (1976; **plate 60**) results from the fusion of an Egyptian hieroglyph of the three-headed serpent and the heads and pendulous breasts of Spero's own invention. In other instances, such as the pistol-wielding figure—derived from the photograph of an Irish Republican Army fighter—that rides the dragon's back, Spero has subtly shifted the signifiers of her pictographic code, redrawing male symbols as female or androgynous ones. And even now that she has, of necessity, turned almost exclusively to reproductive techniques—photo-etched plates and cast rubber stamps—Spero takes full advantage of the broken edges, disintegrating textures, and chromatic elisions of her print media to modify, if not wholly reconceive, source images.

4 Monsters, that is to say unnatural creatures, have always been invented by artists from the deliberately mismatched parts of men or real animals; take demons in Martin Schongauer's engraving *The Temptation of Saint Anthony* (c.1470–75) as one particularly vivid example, or Francisco Goya's *Caprichos* (1799) for another. The principle of "collage" has thus been essential to the poetry of the fantastic as it has been to symbolic and polemical art since long before the advent of "appropriation" or "photomontage." Who is now to say that the hand cannot "think" as well or as self-critically as we can with the camera or the printing press about the complex artifice of representation? The problem may indeed be the reverse. Can any technological means short of computers or video—which are, in a sense, drawing tools—invent forms as various or as unexpected as a draftsman or painter? And is the text or photo work any less a fetish than the handmade picture? In any event, imagination and the capacity for analysis are first vested in the artist, not the means. Certainly, the combination of selecting images and revising them, as Spero does in her 1970s work, represents a notably flexible and fecund synthesis of both approaches.

Spero has thus managed to scavenge through the Imaginary Museum and the public record without succumbing to the temptation of grand larceny, didacticism, or facile irony, while at the same time testing the metamorphic powers of the hand without indulging in stylistic showmanship or rhetorical egocentrism. In so doing, she has restored an emotional urgency and depth to the art of retrieval and commentary. The voices which speak and physical presences which impose themselves are always respected and always polyvalent.

Cultural and class differences are scrupulously observed—never are we asked to accept an individual as a definitive representation of the whole, and never does the artist overshadow her chosen subjects. Yet, neither are they reduced to sociological or ideological ciphers. No trick questions are asked, no "right" answers are provided. Instead, we are obliged to engage with the protagonists of Spero's work on all levels at once—visceral, imaginative, and critical. The anxiety we feel is a product of our awareness of the constant spillage between these different layers of consciousness. And, insofar as Spero does directly intervene, it is to compound that anxiety and prohibit our escape into the security of concentrating on any one dimension of the puzzle she has created at the expense of the others. Driven forward towards an art of commitment and investigation, Spero has, nonetheless, found a way to reach back and incorporate the instinctive responses and procedures which informed her earlier work. To that extent, if in the boys-club context of "Neo-Expressionism" there can be a feminist counterpart or response, Spero's work is it. If not, by maintaining the vital tension between paraphrase and creation, information gathering and evocation, Spero has nonetheless held open the prospect of art of ideas *and* of feeling.

Spero's choice of formats is as crucial to that end as her choice of graphic means. While the 1980s have seen a widespread return to painting on canvas and a concomitant restoration of conservative notions about the preciousness and permanence of the art object, Spero has worked with perishable materials, mounting finished pieces directly on walls with scant regard for their commercial allure. Neither are her scrolls heroic in scale. But they are extensive.

As such, they suggest numerous art historical precedents: Oriental screens and scrolls; classical and pre-classical friezes; the Bayeux Tapestry; the wall posters of Mao's Cultural Revolution; and even the masterwork of Henry Darger, a Chicago recluse whose saga of the Vivian Girls has in its perverse paper-doll scenarios uncanny correspondences with Spero's equally fragile and sometimes equally violent tableaux. But, as apt as these comparisons may at times seem to be, they also tend to obscure Spero's particular accomplishment and motivations. For to a greater or lesser degree all the works just mentioned are narrative. Though in recent pieces such as *Vietnamese Women* (1985; **plates 62–63**) Spero has used repeated images to animate a sequence much as was done in the Persian Lion Hunt reliefs at the British Museum, overall Spero's work has seldom been concerned with live action. Likewise, though most of her larger works may be thought of as "codices"—that is to say, chronicles or histories—none of Spero's scrolls unfold in a strictly linear fashion. Instead, they constitute a variably paced and intricately constructed dialectic of parallel or competing discourses. Fracturing the unity of the focused "picture," Spero's work requires a constant readjustment to disparate detail and alternative methods of exposition. However fixating any particular image may be, one is always aware of something happening adjacent to, ahead of, or behind it.

In numerous forms such disjunctive syntax has been a staple of vanguard art from Cubism, Futurism, and Dada on down to its present variants in appropriative art. But if the discovery of simultaneity began as a celebration of the dynamic confusion of the machine age, in the latter part of the twentieth century it has devolved into an enervated fascination with supposedly incommensurable incidents and deracinated symbols. Millennial modernism, we are told, has spent itself not in a bang but an electronic whimper. History has failed to come to an end and none of its "great narratives" have produced the expected climax at the expected time. Diffused—or defused—into the numbing atmosphere of an external media moment, it has succumbed to a "post-modern" entropy. This is a neat and certainly catchy solution to the problem. And a convenient one for those who, all in decrying the arrogance of mastery, nonetheless fantasize a totalized reality telescoped into the terms of their own circumscribed experience and faddish doctrines.

Painting understood as a self-contained universe has—not necessarily, but in practice—become the emblem of this limitation.[5] Whether vacant or filled to overflowing, the easel picture is problematic insofar as it proposes any absolute view of the world, be it a perfectly static system or a "perfect" chaos. Unwilling to accept either of these options, Spero has attacked the framework which seems to impose them. Exploding the picture plane in all directions, she has allowed her pieces to stretch vertically or horizontally at will, as if the axes of the grid had at last been freed from the closed frontiers of the stretcher. Further, she has with equal determination attacked the architectonic strictures of conventional mural painting, bridging corners with her graphic ribbons and impressing her images directly across the naked surface of the wall.

The formal possibilities suggested by this approach are clearly not confined to the particular uses to which Spero has put them. Yet they are inextricably linked to convictions regarding freedom of visual and imaginative movement and our unrealized capacity to comprehend and synthesize multiple points of view that are central to her purpose. Figurative in its primary aspect, Spero's art is most original and most eloquent in the implications of its abstract logic. And most positive. For, despite the anguish of much of its explicit content, Spero's work offers a concept of the artistic enterprise that is quite literally open-ended. Augmenting the feminist notion of "layering" with that of peripheral vision, Spero reminds us that our discovery of a work, like our exploration of reality, is not predetermined; and that we may at any point be called

5 This is not a simple matter, and I do not mean to suggest that all painting errs equally in this respect. But it is a crucial issue. After all, even the New York School "big picture," despite its attempts to expand beyond the limits of the domestic decoration or "window" on the world-painting of the past, was nonetheless scaled to the gesture of the artists and focused by that gesture. The experience of a Pollock or a de Kooning thus remains a one-on-one exchange between viewer and the creator. The problem is how to design and fill a format that is more centrifugal than centripetal, yet capable of organizing images or visual incidents. Environmental sculpture has addressed this issue by taking David Smith's open-core concept of sculptural structure and dispersing subordinate plans and volumes still further into space. Painting and drawing have proven more conservative. Jonathan Borofsky—not incidentally a socially conscious artist who matured in the aftermath of the 1960s—has suggested some possibilities. Nancy Spero suggests others.

upon to redirect our attention, retrace our steps, leap forward or lead back, and begin again; and that it is by virtue of such unbounded access and such unrestricted demands upon our ability to rethink our experience that we remain at liberty.

Ignored by most and type-cast by others as *political*, *feminist*, a *seventies* artist, etc., it is thus Spero's hard-won privilege not only to interrupt and dispute the present discourse on "closure," but to show by example how such closure can be avoided. To turn again to Spero now is not merely to pay homage to a career, but to attend to the paradoxical optimism her work embodies. Delving in the past while simultaneously speculating on the future course of her society and the possibilities of her medium, Spero's has been and is an art of "recovery"—and always an art of resistance.

The Weapon and the Wound

First published in Leon Golub and Robert Storr, Nancy Spero. The War Series, 1966–1970*, exh. cat. (Charta, Milan, 2003), pp.9–13. This is the catalogue of the exhibition of the same title held at Galerie Lelong, New York in 2003 and at Galerie Lelong, Paris in 2004.*

Far away, they are fighting. Close to home, they are repackaging the mess. We've been through this before, too many times not to know in our gut what is actually going on and where, swiftly and horribly, or with interminable but equally disastrous slowness, it will lead. Nevertheless, it is becoming increasingly easy to lose our hold on events. In fact, everything we see conspires to make it so, since the images that bring us the news of war, or rather the images that substitute themselves for its reality, have changed radically in recent years.

Of course, war has always been photogenic. And those photos have always been manipulated. From nineteenth-century views of Crimean battlefields littered with cannonballs and Pennsylvania farmlands dotted with corpses in picturesque spasms—Civil War photographers such as Mathew Brady routinely repositioned the dead for dramatic impact—to twentieth-century reportage of the World Wars, in which cropping refined the abstract compositional qualities of shots taken in the heat of action and darkroom techniques enhanced their chiaroscuro effects, men and women with cameras have found beauty in destruction and artfully improved upon it.[1] Yet, never have depictions of the dirty business of killing on command been so clean and well designed as now. This reflects a growing reluctance on the part of officials to allow reporters to record the conflict firsthand. For the most part, "embedded" with military units in the rear of the war, correspondents are granted limited access to the front, lest they see things and show us things—charred bodies of the enemy blasted beyond recognition by "surgical strikes" and "smart bombs," the agonizing bodies of casualties on our side, or the look of fear or frustration on the faces of our own troops—that might give even the most gung-ho citizen pause.

Cartoons now replace documentation. The current one is our first digitally animated war. It has been a long time coming, but in the months between 9/11 and the invasion of Iraq, examples have popped up everywhere with accelerated frequency. On airport news racks, for instance, amid the lifestyle magazines appeared a special issue of *Popular Science* devoted to the "Twenty-first-century Soldier." Bound

1 Editor's note: Mathew Brady (1822–1896), American photographer.

in glossy black with the picture of a futuristic infantryman aiming his weapon straight at the reader, it is filled with slick promotional photos of heavy armaments and computer-generated scenes of guns firing, rockets launching, and laser-equipped space stations knocking out missiles in the upper atmosphere. The armed forces and their suppliers produce and distribute to the media and to recruits still more sophisticated DVDs that illustrate the new strategies and the new technologies of combat. In these 3-D simulations, robotic figures clad in Spandex-like uniforms move through postcard wastelands and cities not yet laid to waste, shooting guns that emit neat beams of light that, just as neatly, vaporize their targets. No bloodletting. No cries. Just specters of "them" and specters of "us;" and in the end we are the only fictions still standing. In the saturation coverage of the war—the information equivalent of saturation bombing with the significantly different mandate to "soothe and awe"—you will no doubt have seen some of these sequences on a screen behind expert commentators who mimic meteorologists describing weather patterns. They are the middlemen between correspondents, who are not quite on site, and the military planners, who are, as always, safely out of sight.

This modernizing, streamlining, and sanitizing of violence is the by-product of a thousand video games and movie morphings. Or perhaps such entertainments are the real products after all, the secret purpose of an industry of push-button mayhem for which murderous distractions are simultaneously a series of laboratory experiments, a financial resource, and a peacetime cover. In any case, they have altered forever what war looks like at a distance and perhaps what it looks like up close as well—at least until it explodes in your face.

Made between 1966 and 1970 in response to the Unites States' escalating involvement in Vietnam, Nancy Spero's the *War Series* (1966–70; **plates 8–18, 20**) presents a very different picture of mechanized ferocity, but the graphic competition it now faces is the seamless version that has recently asserted its hegemony. Because her images are no more factual that theirs, nor are they any less a matter of self-consciously constructed signs deployed in syntactic combinations or phrases that "mean" things they cannot fully embody. Indeed, among the distinctive aspects of Spero's work was her prematurely postmodern recognition of the semiotics of picture-making. I say "prematurely postmodern" only to signal the discrepancy between Spero's early understanding and use of linguistic concepts, and the general dissemination of structuralism and post-structuralist concepts in the 1970s and 1980s, a discrepancy which explains why she is so seldom mentioned in the literature of the field. That is the fate of precursors who survive to become the contemporaries of younger artists styled as the personification of the new. Spero's exposure to critical thought, and its French component in particular, began in Paris where she lived and worked in the years leading up to making the *War Series*. A trace, quite literally, of this milieu is found in her gouache-and-ink-on-paper *Les bourgeois passent...* (1968; **plate 21**), which incorporates a sentence culled from Jean Genet's 1943 novel *Notre-Dame-des-Fleurs* (Our Lady of the Flowers) that reads: "Les bourgeois passent, font la foule, et ne voient rien, ne savent rien, à peine sont-ils insensiblement déplacés dans leur calme état de confiance par ce rien" (The bourgeois file by, make a crowd, and see nothing, know nothing; in their calm state of confidence, they are scarcely sensitive to being displaced by this nothing). It is to that unshakable inattention and indifference that Spero's work in its entirety is addressed.

In Paris she also discovered the writings of Antonin Artaud, perpetual insurgent against the tyranny of language and diabolical engineer of its implosion.[2] Transcribing excerpts from his essays, manifestos, and poems onto white expanses of paper (**plates 22–27**) studded with her own intensely worked hieroglyphic emblems of gagging, screaming heads, bodies in alternately articulate and inarticulate paroxysms, and monstrous creatures that recast the antique iconography of the grotesque in mutable forms, Spero devised a unique interchange between text and image. Spero's *Codex Artaud* (1971–72; **plates 28–29, 30–31, 32, 33, 34**) is the culmination of this effort to treat pictures as utterances and words as icons in a dizzyingly open-ended flow of polymorphous and polyvalent signs. Anyone wishing to correct the diminished role still commonly accorded women artists in the 1960s and,

2 Antonin Artaud (1896–1948), French poet, playwright, stage and film actor, director, and visual artist.

at the same time, ground the post-formalist esthetic in a practical and theoretical grasp of the emerging discourses of the period would do well to start with this extraordinary thirty-two-part work.

The *War Series* anticipates the *Codex Artaud* but is different in appearance as well as in substance. Different, too, are the expectations brought to them, given their subject matter. Whereas *Codex Artaud* deals in archetypes, the *War Series* takes current events as its point of departure. Moreover, it protests the causes and consequences of those events. As such, it falls, or seems to fall, into a category of art for which authenticity and expressivity are the ultimate criteria—in short, the art of moral witness. Francisco Goya's *The Disasters of War* (1810–20; **plate 37**) is the highest achievement and most frequently referred to model of this genre. In a suite of eighty-three etchings and aquatints, Goya portrayed the atrocities and degradation of Napoleon's army as it marched through Spain. The supreme historical irony of the situation was that to Goya and other liberals, Napoleon stood for modernity in contrast to the corruption and superstition in which his monarchist, priest-ridden nation was mired. With a dreadful sense of purpose, Enlightenment on the march brought even greater darkness than had existed before, and under cover of that darkness, its uniformed representatives indulged in wholesale slaughter. In much of the art labeled Goyaesque these political contradictions are reduced to a simplistic Manichaean opposition of the forces of good and evil, the latter a valuable though problematic word whose use is being denied us through its constant reiteration by propagandists. But the feeling of betrayal that informs Goya's series is an indispensable element of its meaning. His anger and his sorrow are directed not only at "crimes against humanity," the inevitable cruelty of war, and perhaps the inherent sadism of humankind, but also at the perversion of a social and political ideal. After all of the torture he describes, the abiding disaster is this laying waste to hope in a world where its roots were already too desperately shallow.

To an even greater extent than Goya's, Spero's war cycle is predicated on an essentialized notion of human nature, and a gendered one at that. Some of the titles make this explicit and specifically identify war with masculine violence. *Male Bomb*, *Sperm Bomb* (both 1966;

respectively **plates 11** and **12**), and *Male Bomb / Swastika* (no longer extant; **plate 18**) are the most declarative in words as well as in pictorial detail: the stiff thrusting penis of the body as mushroom cloud in the first, the mushroom cloud as penis and testicles in the second, and the nude torso with penis capped by a head haloed by a Star of David in the third incarnate and sexualize this destructive drive. As every little boy instinctively understands whether he reaches for them or avoids them, guns are the phallus, but in Spero's post-Hiroshima cosmology of violence, the ultimate phallic power is the ultimate weapon. And all lesser ordinance aspires to its force. *Fuck* (1966), with its B-52-like fuselages resembling aeronautic erections, makes the sexual politics of "conquest" still more obvious, as does *Clown and Helicopter* (1967; **plate 15**). *Bomb Shitting* (1966; **plate 13**) further develops and complicates this metaphoric equation. Here, the annihilating "gift" of the anal sadistic child drops from pink buttocks that double as a scrotum while both the paired heads above and the projectile heads below spew fire or blood like vomit. In this context, *Female Helicopters* (1966) may come as a surprise, until, that is, one looks again at the Janus-like cloud heads just mentioned and recognizes that occasionally in Roman mythology Janus mutates into a feminine form and that the faces of Spero's monsters also resemble Harpies or Furies. *Female Bomb* (1966; **plate 16**) reinforces this correlation and, without direct reference to it, recalls American physicist J. Robert Oppenheimer's spontaneous utterance on witnessing the first Atomic explosion: "Now I have become death, destroyer of worlds." Oppenheimer was the "father" of the Bomb and his paraphrase of the Hindu writing Bhagavad-Gita eliminates specific mention of Shiva, but in the Hindu cosmology to which he was alluding, death also took the form of a woman, Kali, uniting in a feminine deity the giving of life with its taking. The hubris of the nuclear age was for humankind to arrogate to itself the role of ultimate creator and destroyer, and it is to this irony that Spero's archetypal incarnations point. Spero's war machines also resemble insects: a swarm of black flies in *Female Helicopters*; a multi-legged predator in *The Bug, Helicopter, Victim* (from 1966, one of the first in the series; **plate 8**); a wide-eyed, vomiting wasp in *Gunship* (1966), and beetle-like planes in *Gunship and Victims* (1967). Other variants, for example *Victims Thrown From Helicopter* (1968)—a little-discussed way of disposing of captives—and *Helicopter, Victim, Astronaut* (1968; **plate 21**)—which verbally and pictorially collapses the distance between the aerospace industry's two government mandates—use the formal analogy of this insect motif as the basis for the beautiful but also harrowing graphic abbreviations of the classic gunship and rotors. In *Helicopter and Victims* (1967; **plate 19**), Spero turns that shape into a repulsive, defecating slug. The title of a work, not included here [in this exhibition at Galerie Lelong] but also part of the series, *K.I.L.L F.O.R M.O.M* (1966; **plate 14**), is a reminder that the gendering of war is not merely the invention of those who contest it. Tattoos of this sort do show up on the arms of young men sent out to defend the "motherland," though in the new "coeducational" army one wonders if this custom has changed or in some fashion mutated on the bare skin of women recruits, with the "fatherland" always being the patriarchal option, though one inseparable from its Nazi past.

That Nazi past is also very much in evidence in these paintings. Adolf Eichmann's trial in 1961 and the concentration camp trials that followed in the first half of the decade were a jolting amplification of public awareness of the persecution of the Jews. This dovetailed with a gradual awakening to the fact that, even if the victimization of the Jews was unique among the genocides of modern history, terrorism in the guise of conventional warfare was hardly a thing of the past. Any nation was susceptible to the temptation, from the French in Algeria and Indochina to the North Americans in Vietnam. Thus, while no serious artist—and certainly no Jewish artist, as Spero is—would mistake the United States' conduct of the war in Southeast Asia for the Holocaust, the distance separating the massacres at My Lai and Lidice is too narrow to ignore. Although the shame of My Lai was still several years in the future when Spero completed the last of these drawings, they have the aspect of a premonition, and by the mid-1970s images of Vietnamese civilians pulped on the ground that were reminiscent of My Lai photographs were a regular feature of Spero's work. The crux of the matter is not one of establishing an arbitrary congruence between two incommensurable systems—Hitler's Reich and Kennedy, Johnson, and Nixon's Republic—but rather of the potential or actual eruption of the fascist impulse in any society that regards its adversaries, and even its allies of convenience, as innately alien. What motivated the *War Series* then was not an abstract preoccupation with the "human condition" at its worst, but a historically informed alertness to a present, politically charged danger. The danger was that we, as a nation, blinded by the certainty of our own virtue and by the ideology of American exceptionalism, would plunge at least partway down the calamitous path trod by our Second World War enemies. Spero's *War Series* was prompted, therefore, not only by a general aversion to militarism but also, in quite specific political circumstances, by the sting of promises broken, principles overturned, and the failure of a society to live by its own ideals. Spero's at once harsh and evanescent paintings on paper are stylistically unlike Goya's dense, gritty etchings—if anything, she seems to have taken her inspiration from the ink drawings and watercolors made by Japanese survivors of the United States' first use of atomic weapons. Nevertheless, apart from such formal differences, these two bodies of work have this in common: both are bitter testaments of disillusionment.

There is another significant distinction between the *War Series* and *The Disasters of War* to be underscored as well. Under a scene of refugees fleeing the advance of Napoleon's troops, Goya inscribed onto the plate the simple statement, "This I saw," and on the next plate in the series, "And this too." Spero, of course, did not see the strafing and napalming of Vietnamese villages firsthand. Rather, she interpreted what everyone then saw in newspapers, in magazines, and on the nightly news, and reduced that flood of images to their sickening essentials, to indelible emblems of violence. Her work acknowledged the impossibility of "bringing the war home" in its details but made clear that the naked moral and political terms of the United States' Southeast Asian adventure were inescapable.

That was decades ago. Now, to a far greater extent than ever, information is hoarded, reprocessed, and doled out only when it is useful to those who control it, and only when it has been made presentable to citizens who, for reasons of state and profit, are treated as mere consumers. Or it is manufactured. The sophistication with which this is currently being done must not be underestimated if there is to be any hope of countering its effects. Nor can it be expected that periodic injections of uncensored "reality" will be sufficient to break the thrall of staged or simulated combat and hyped or faked victory. This is not the Information Age; it is the Disinformation Age. Big lies need last only as long as it takes to complete the missions for which they serve as alibis. Then a new one is put into circulation in synch with a new mission.

The truth of the situation with which we are faced exceeds the verifiable facts, and the facts are too easily contested or contradicted, or simply neutralized by fictions masquerading as facts, for there to be any chance of definitively setting the empirical record straight. Instead, what is needed is an alternative lexicon of signs that represent the fundamental dynamics of war in the age of technological superworks—of which one is, of course, unrivaled—and their ideologies of might and right. This is what Spero saw in the mid-1960s. The *War Series* she made then marks a prescient shift from a veristic mode to a semiotic one, speaking truth to power without recourse to the earnest naturalism that typifies but also belies so much protest art. In the *War Series*, she achieved this by forging her own symbols and giving her own names to the things that power sought to obscure through its euphemisms of triumphant efficiency and inscrutable otherness. That is the challenge today, and, in conjunction with the larger critical and artistic enterprise of which they are a part, these paintings provide an invaluable lesson in how it can be done and with what urgency and passion the codes of an innovative post-structuralist art can be imbued.

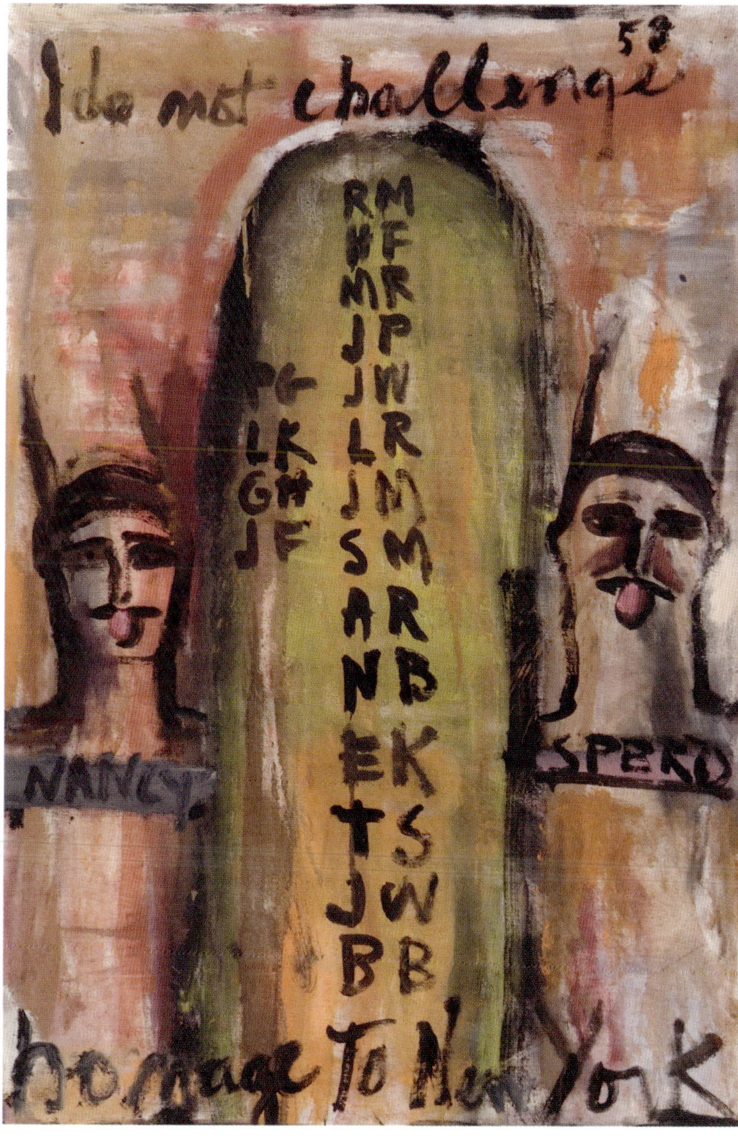

1
Homage to New York (I Do Not Challenge), 1958
Oil on canvas, 119.4 × 78.7 cm (47 × 31 in.)

Minneapolis Institute of Art. The Mary Ingebrand-Pohlad Endowment for Twentieth Century Paintings and gift of various donors, by exchange
Photo courtesy Galerie Lelong, New York

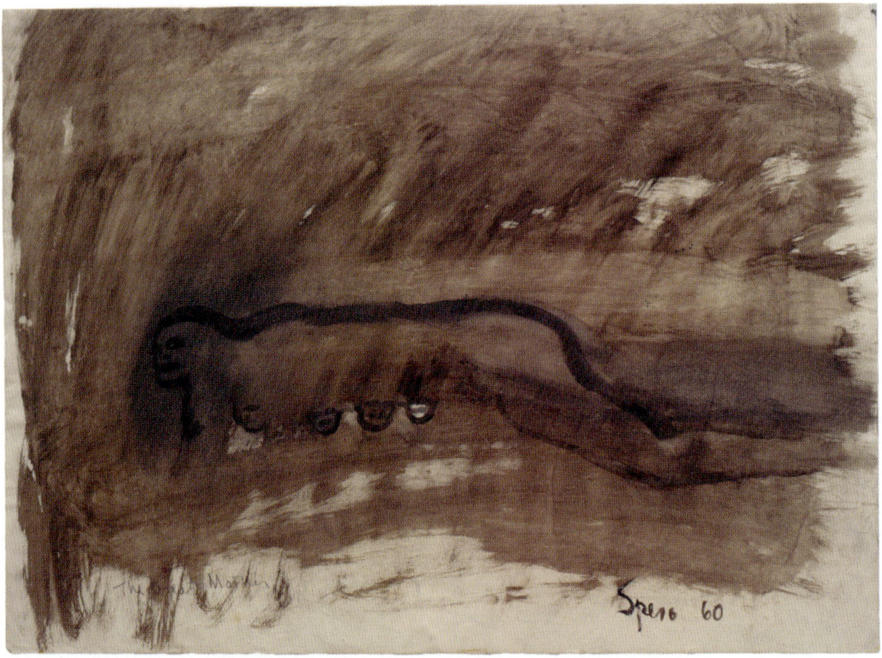

2
The Great Mother, 1960
Ink on paper, 40.6 × 55.9 (16 × 22 in.)

Pennsylvania Academy of the Fine Arts,
Philadelphia. John S. Phillips Art Fund
Photo courtesy Galerie Lelong, New York

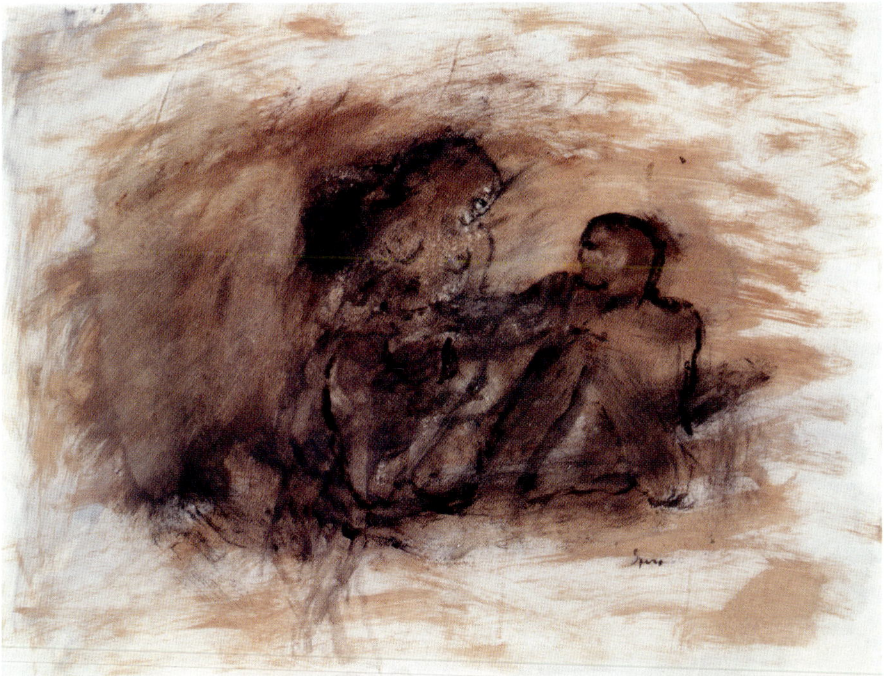

3
Le Couple (Lovers), 1960
Gouache and ink on paper,
43.8 × 55.8 cm (17 ¼ × 22 in.)

Collection Dan Miller, New York
Photo: David Reynolds. Courtesy The Nancy Spero and Leon Golub Foundation for the Arts

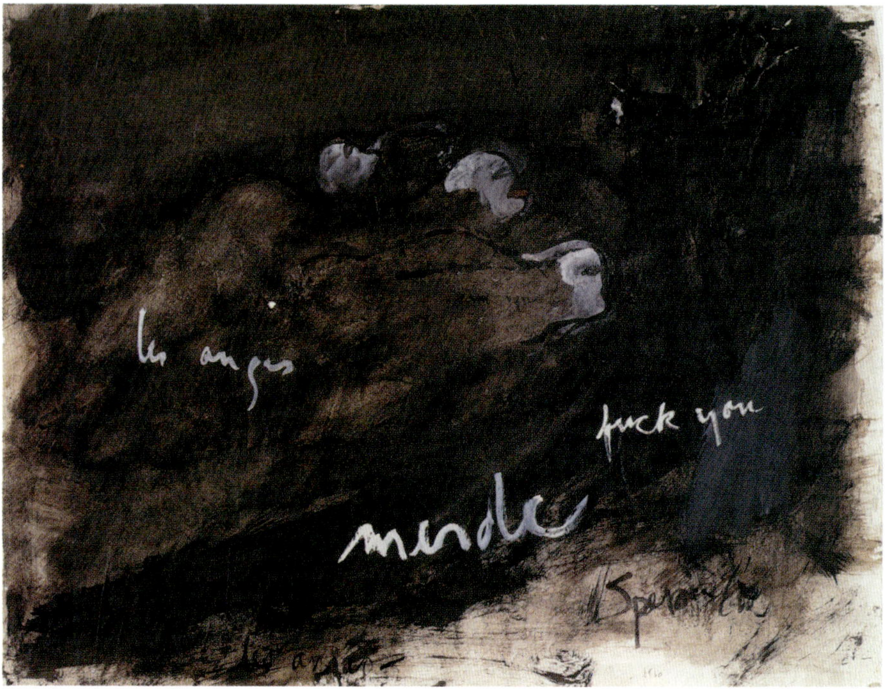

4
Les Anges, Merde, Fuck You, 1960
Gouache and ink on paper,
43.8 × 55.9 cm (17 ¼ × 22 in.)

Collection Philip Golub
Photo courtesy Galerie Lelong, New York

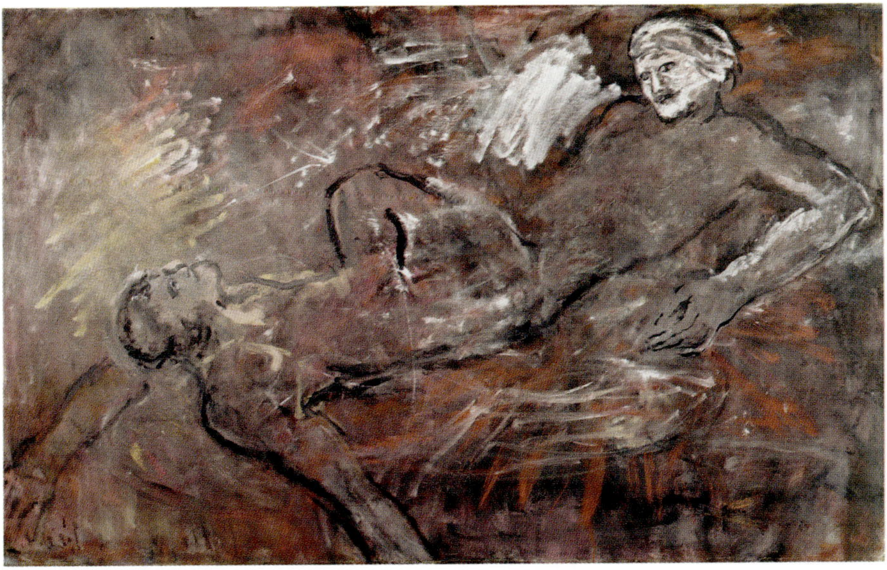

5
Le Couple (Lovers), 1964
Oil on canvas, 130 × 203 cm
(51 3⁄16 × 79 15⁄16 in.)

Collection Camille and Paul Oliver-Hoffmann, Chicago
Photo: David Reynolds. Courtesy The Nancy Spero and Leon Golub Foundation for the Arts

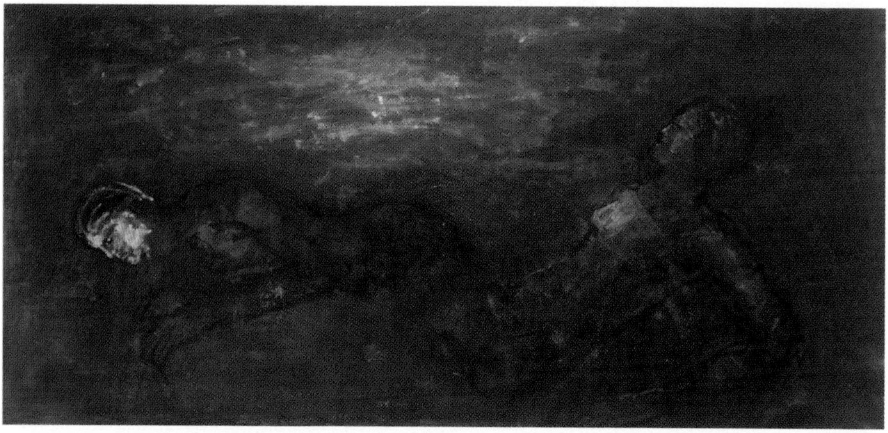

6
Le Couple (Lovers VII), 1964
Oil on canvas,
96.5 × 198.1 cm (38 × 78 in.)

National Gallery of Canada, Ottawa. Purchased 2004
Photo courtesy Galerie Lelong, New York

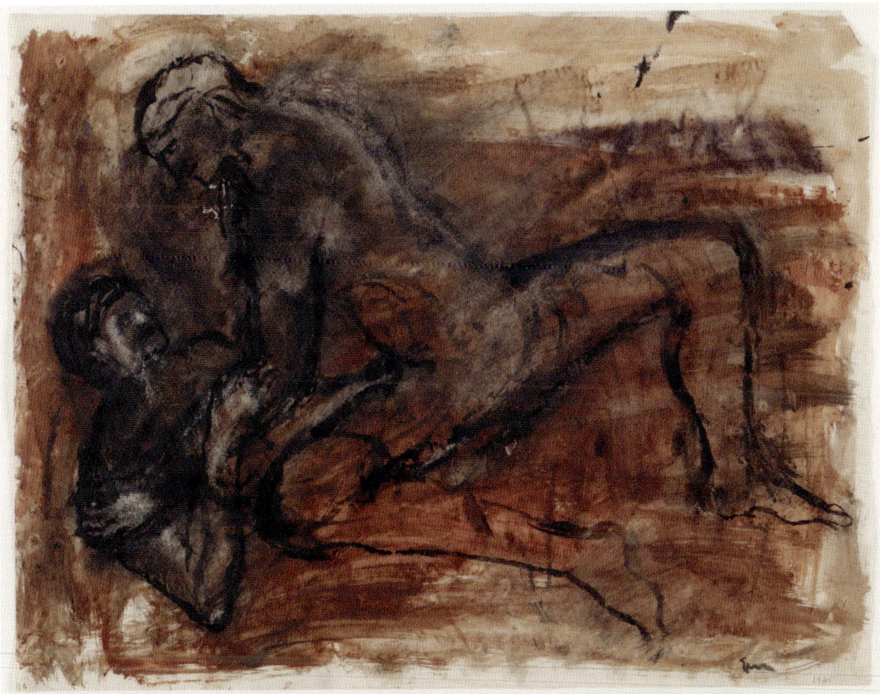

7
Lovers, 1965
Watercolor on paper,
47.6 × 60.3 cm (18 ¾ × 23 ¾ in.)

Photo courtesy Galerie Lelong, New York

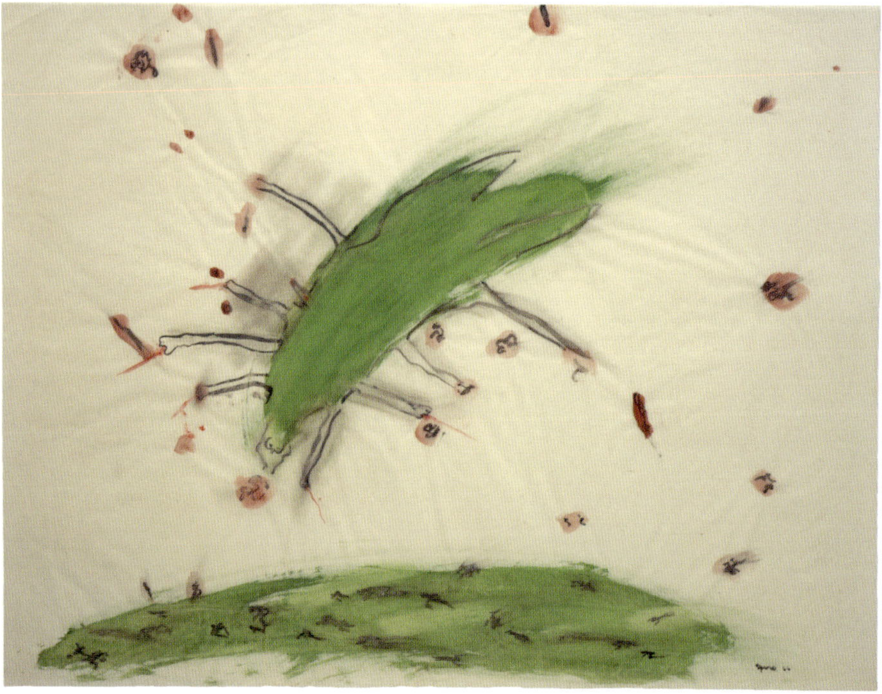

8
The Bug, Helicopter, Victim, from the *War Series*, 1966
Gouache and ink on paper, 48.3 × 59.1 cm (19 × 23 ¼ in.)

Pennsylvania Academy of the Fine Arts,
Philadelphia. John S. Phillips Art Fund
Photo courtesy Galerie Lelong, New York

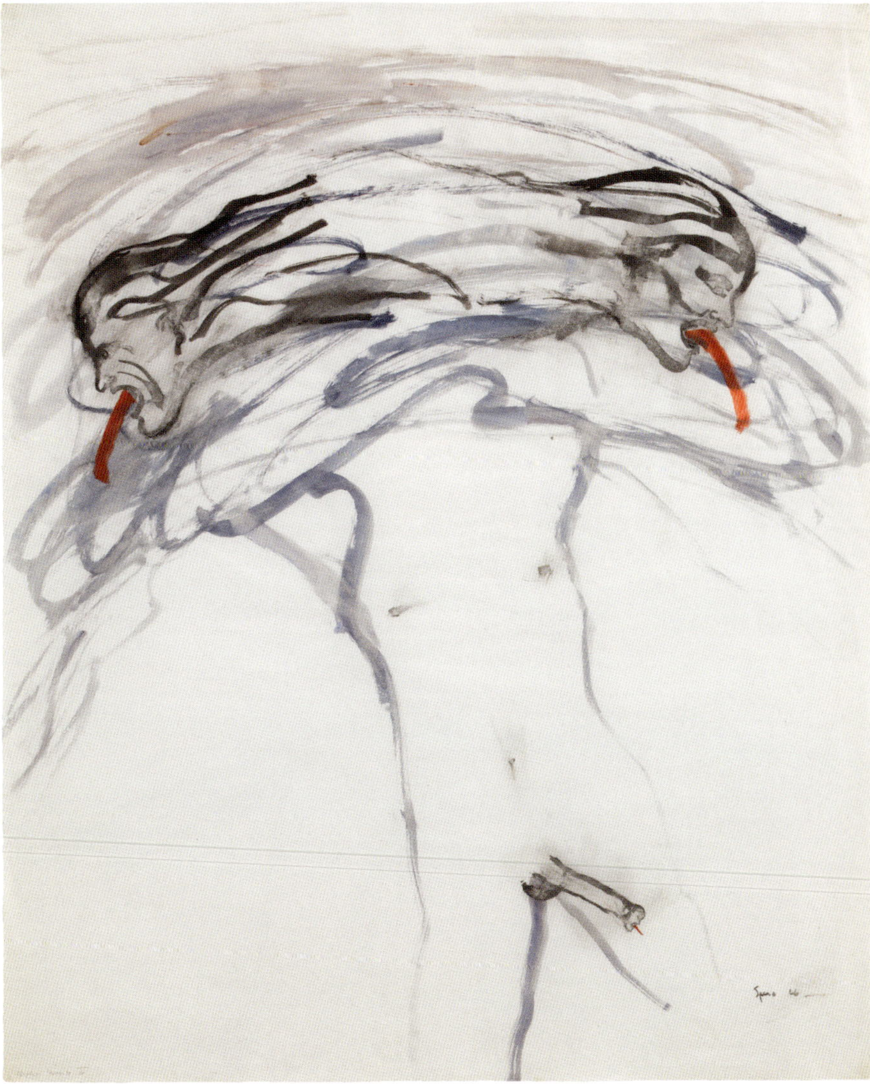

9
Male Bomb I, from the *War Series*, 1966
Gouache and ink on paper,
86.4 × 68.6 cm (34 × 27 in.)

Photo courtesy Galerie Lelong, New York

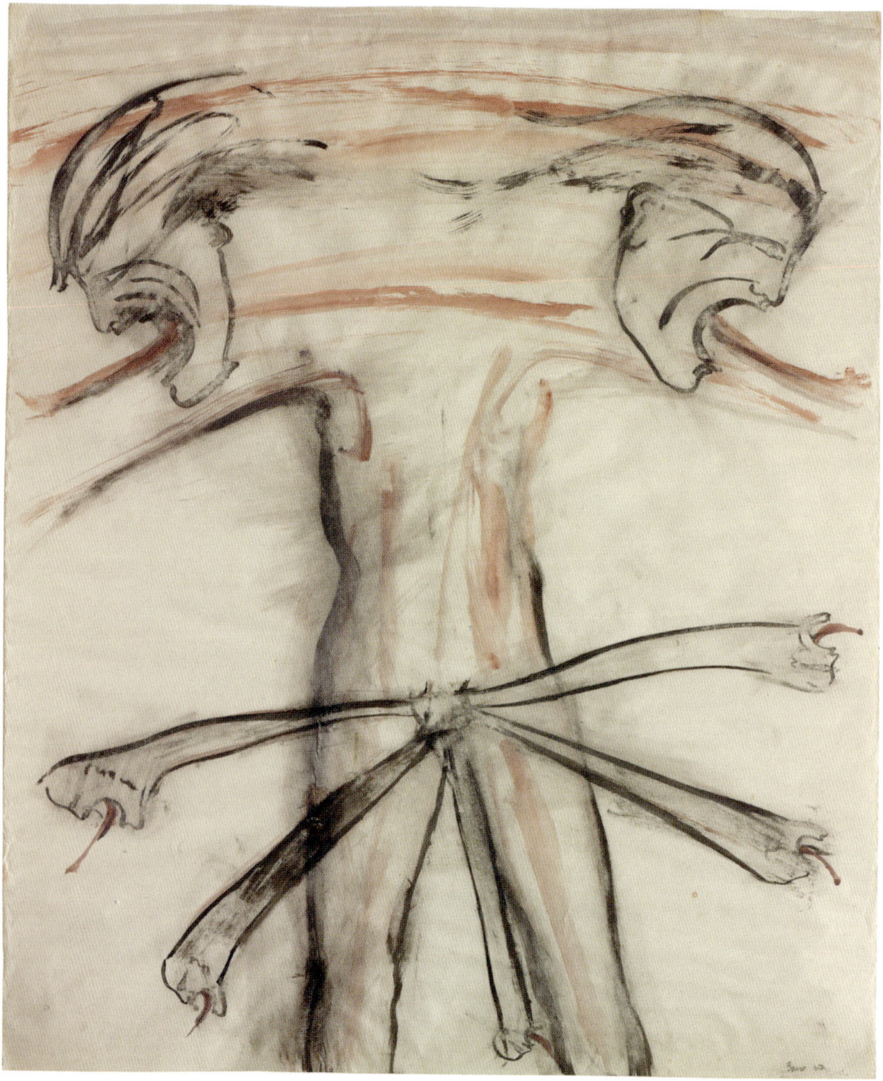

10
Male Bomb, from the *War Series*, 1966
Gouache and ink on paper,
86 × 69 cm (33 ⅞ × 27 $^{3}/_{16}$ in.)

Louisiana Museum of Modern Art, Humlebæk, Denmark.
Acquired with funding from The Augustinus Foundation
Photo courtesy Galerie Lelong, New York

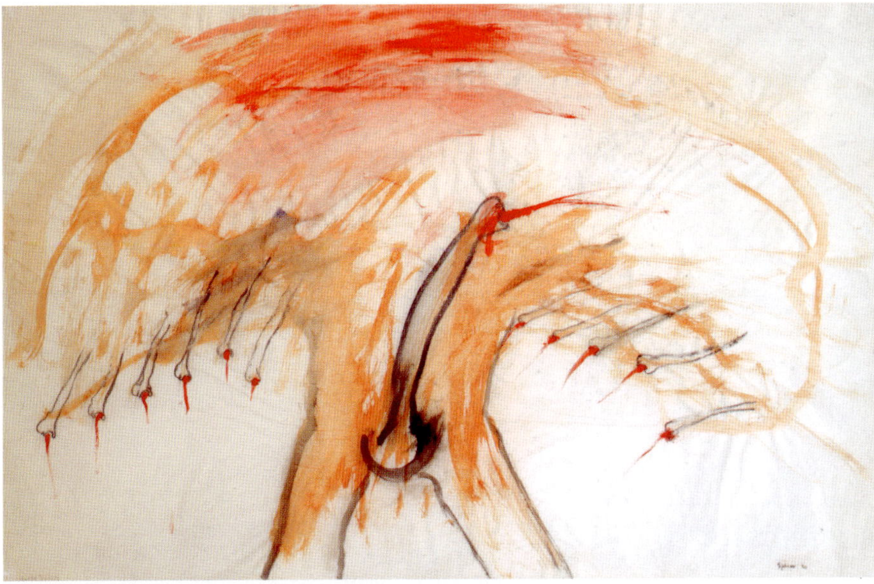

11
Male Bomb, from the *War Series*, 1966
Gouache on paper,
68.5 × 86.3 cm (27 × 34 in.)

Photo: David Reynolds. Courtesy The Nancy Spero and Leon Golub Foundation for the Arts

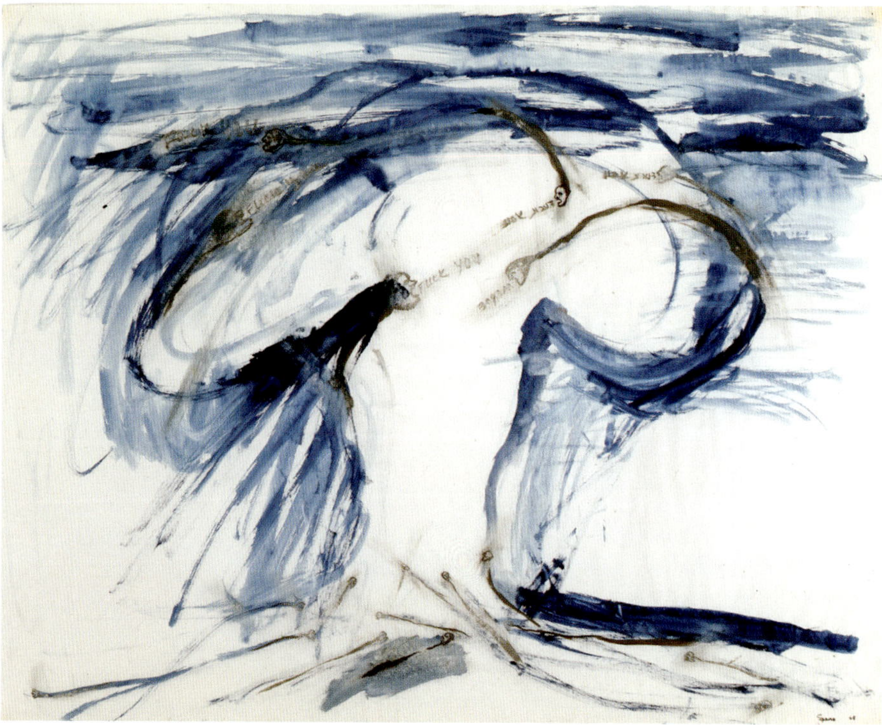

12
Sperm Bomb, from the *War Series*, 1966
Gouache and ink on paper,
68.6 × 86.4 cm (27 × 34 in.)

Weatherspoon Art Museum, The University of North Carolina at Greensboro. Museum purchase with funds from the Jefferson-Pilot Endowment, the Burlington Industries Endowment and the Weatherspoon Art Museum Acquisition Endowment, 2003
Photo courtesy Galerie Lelong, New York

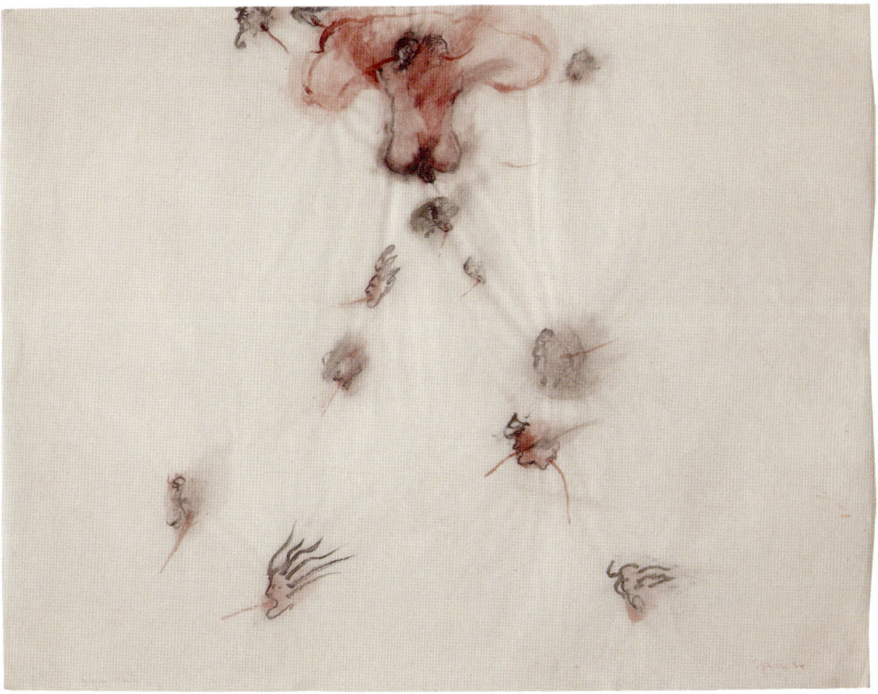

13
Bomb Shitting, from the *War Series*, 1966
Gouache and ink on paper,
47.6 × 60.3 cm (18 ¾ × 23 ¾ in.)

Museo Nacional Centro de Arte Reina Sofia, Madrid
Archivo Fotográfico Museo Nacional Centro de Arte Reina Sofía

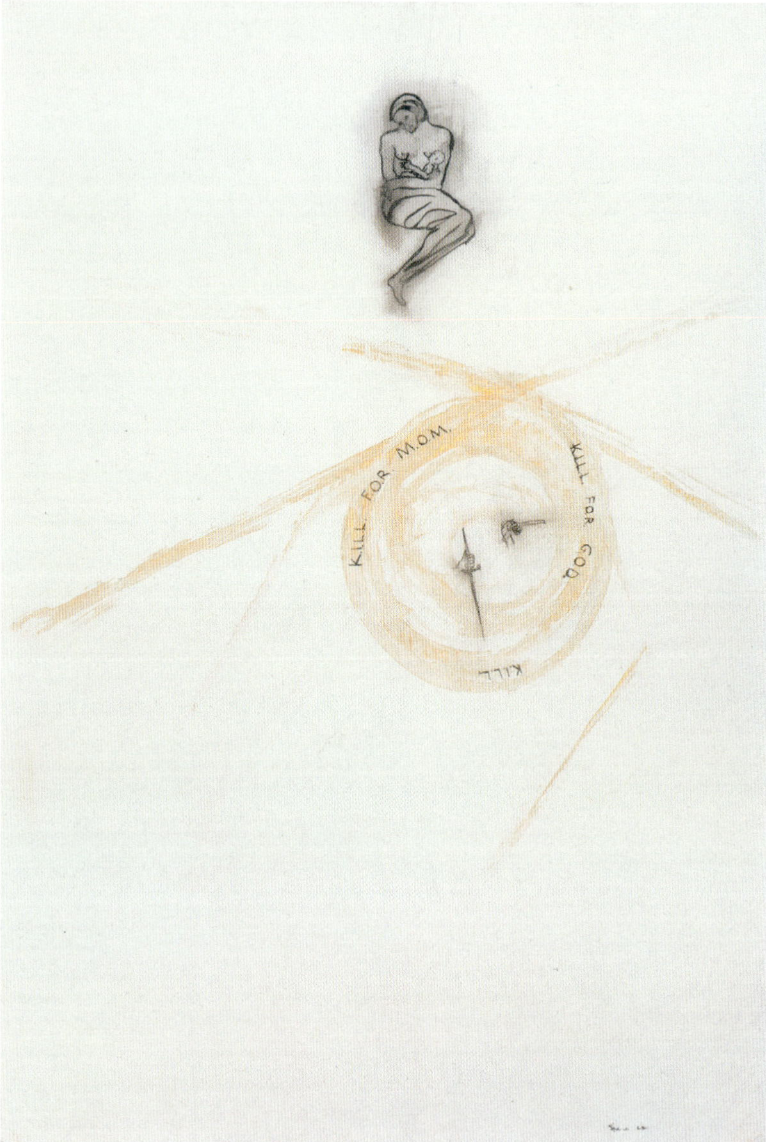

14
K.I.L.L F.O.R M.O.M, from the *War Series*, 1966
Gouache and ink on paper,
91.4 × 60.1 cm (36 × 24 in.)

Private Collection
Photo courtesy Galerie Lelong, New York

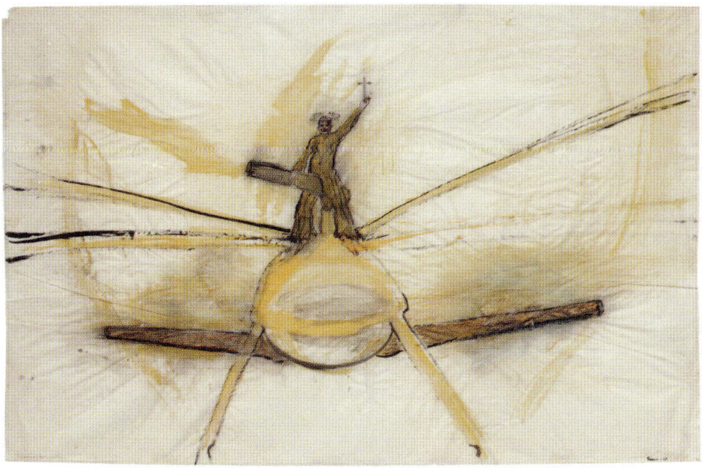

15
Clown and Helicopter, from the *War Series*, 1967
Gouache and ink on paper,
61 × 91.4 cm (24 × 36 in.)

Museo Nacional Centro de Arte Reina Sofia, Madrid
Archivo Fotográfico Museo Nacional Centro de Arte Reina Sofía

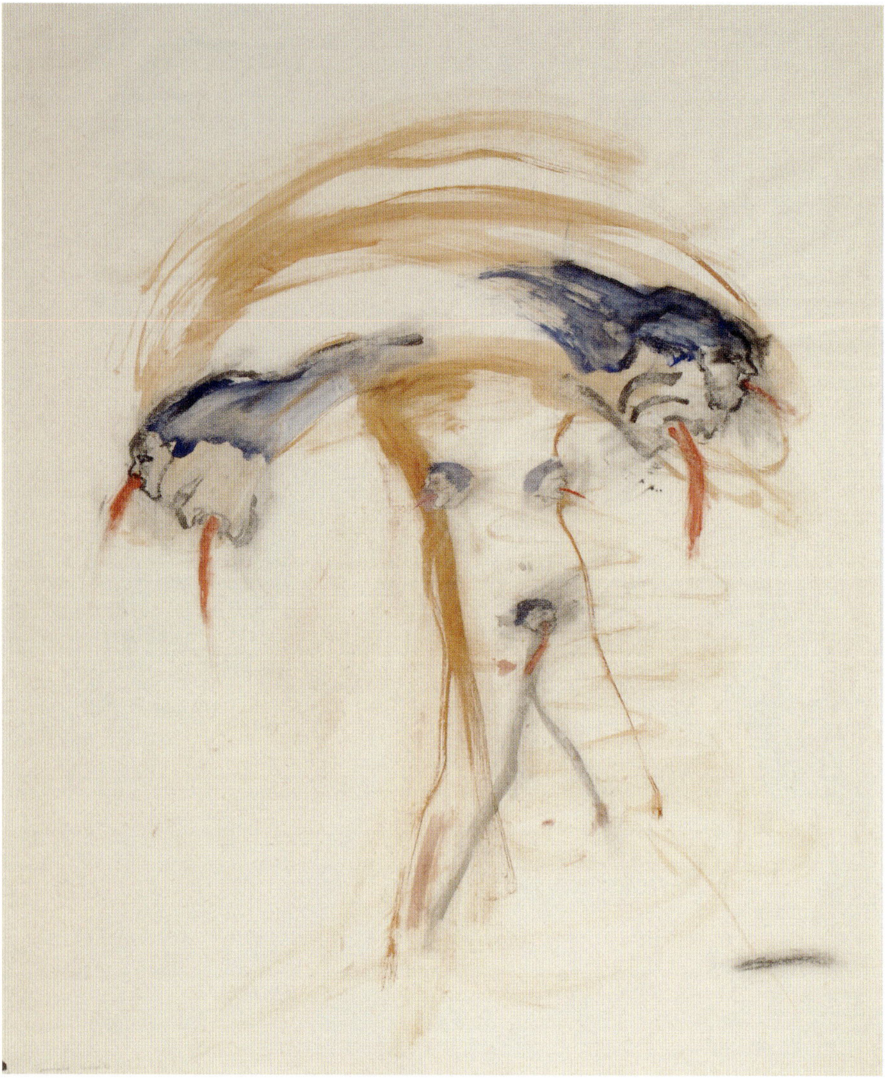

16
Female Bomb, from the *War Series*, 1966
Gouache and ink on paper, 86.4 × 69.2 cm (34 × 27 ¼ in.)

ICA, Boston. Gift of Barbara Lee, The Barbara Lee Collection of Art by Women
Photo courtesy Galerie Lelong, New York

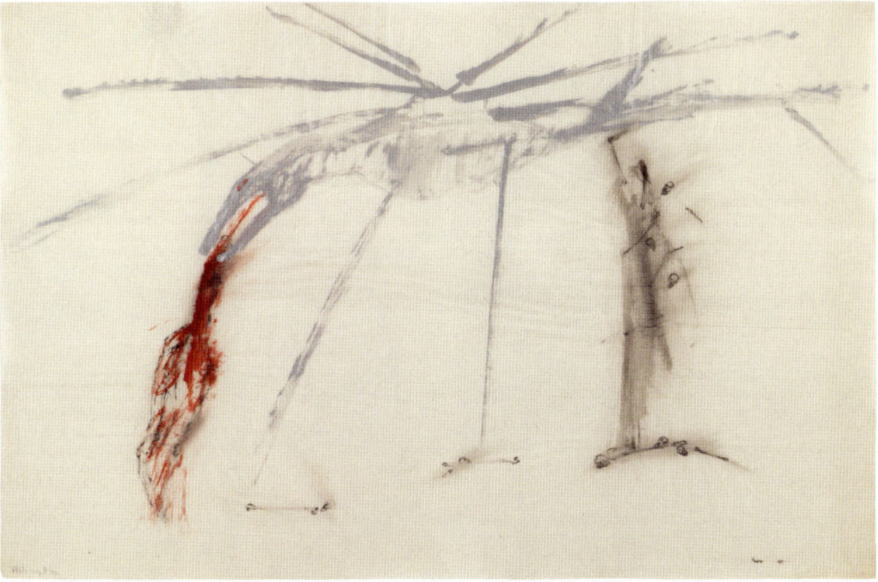

17
Helicopter and Victims, from the *War Series*, 1967
Gouache and ink on paper, 61 × 91.4 cm (24 × 36 in.)

The Stephen Golub Fine Arts Trust
Photo courtesy Galerie Lelong, New York

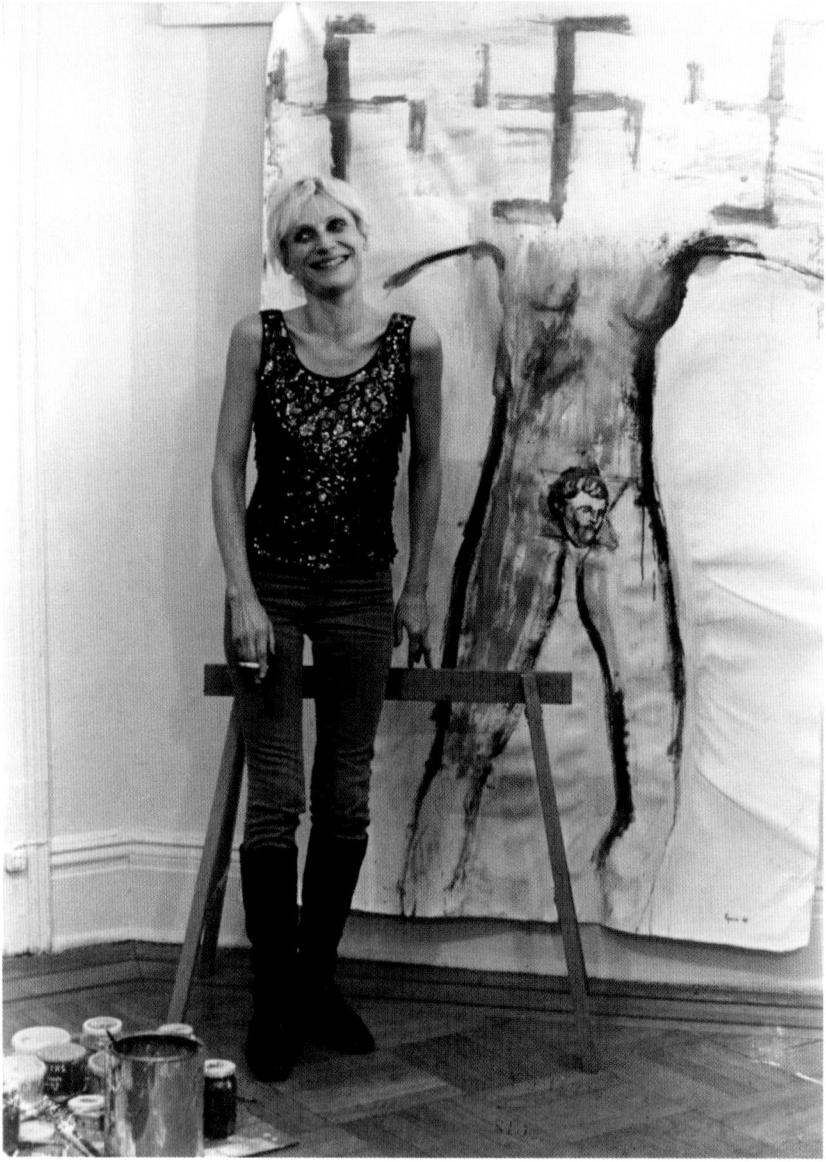

18
Nancy Spero in the studio with destroyed *War Painting* (1968)

Photo courtesy Galerie Lelong, New York

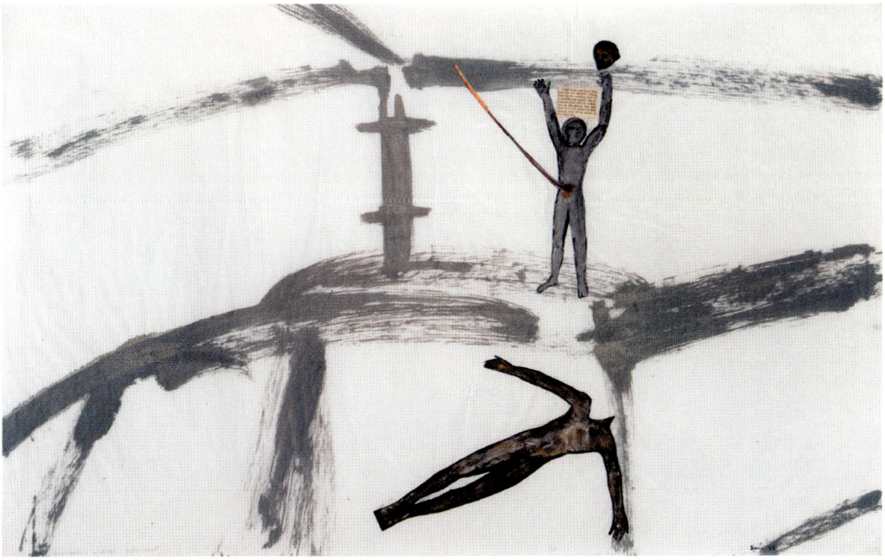

19
Helicopter, Victim, Astronaut,
from the *War Series*, 1968
Gouache, ink, and collage on paper,
63.5 × 100.3 cm (25 × 39 ½ in.)

Pérez Art Museum Miami. Museum purchase
with funds provided by the Helena Rubinstein
Philanthropic Fund at The Miami Foundation
Photo courtesy Galerie Lelong, New York

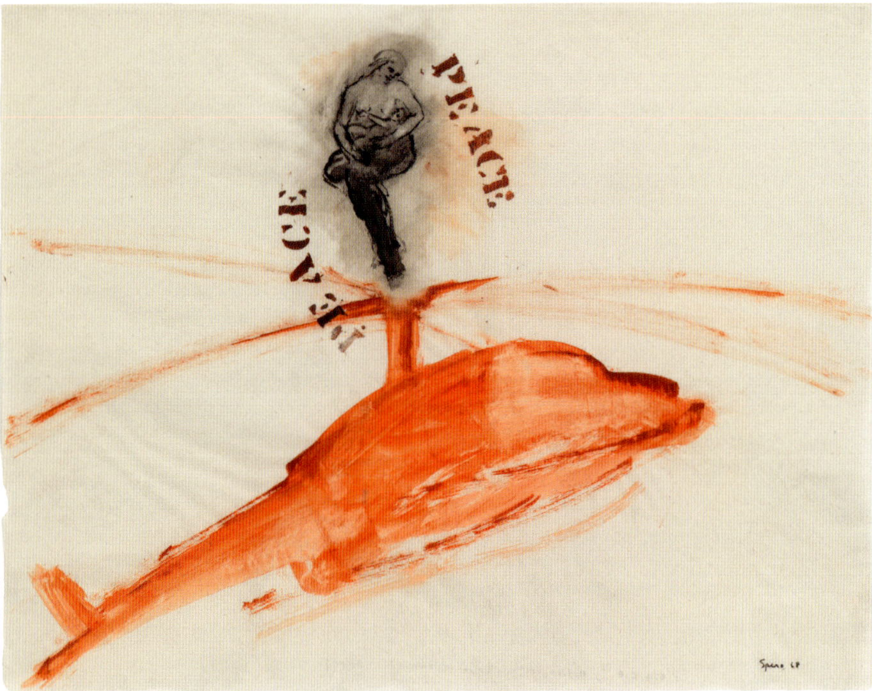

20
P.E.A.C.E., Helicopter, Mother + Children, from the *War Series*, 1968
Gouache and ink on paper, 48 × 61 cm (19 × 24 in.)

Minneapolis Institute of Art. Gift of funds from Mary and Bob Mersky
Photo courtesy Galerie Lelong, New York

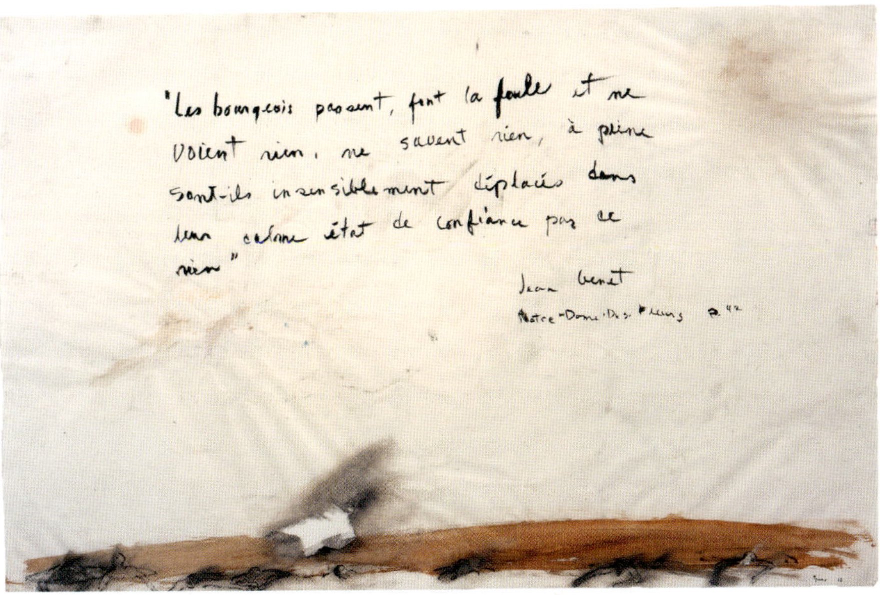

21
Les bourgeois passent..., 1968
Gouache and ink on paper,
61 × 91.4 cm (24 × 36 in.)

Centre Georges Pompidou, Paris. Gift of Philip S. Golub, 2011
Photo courtesy Galerie Lelong, New York

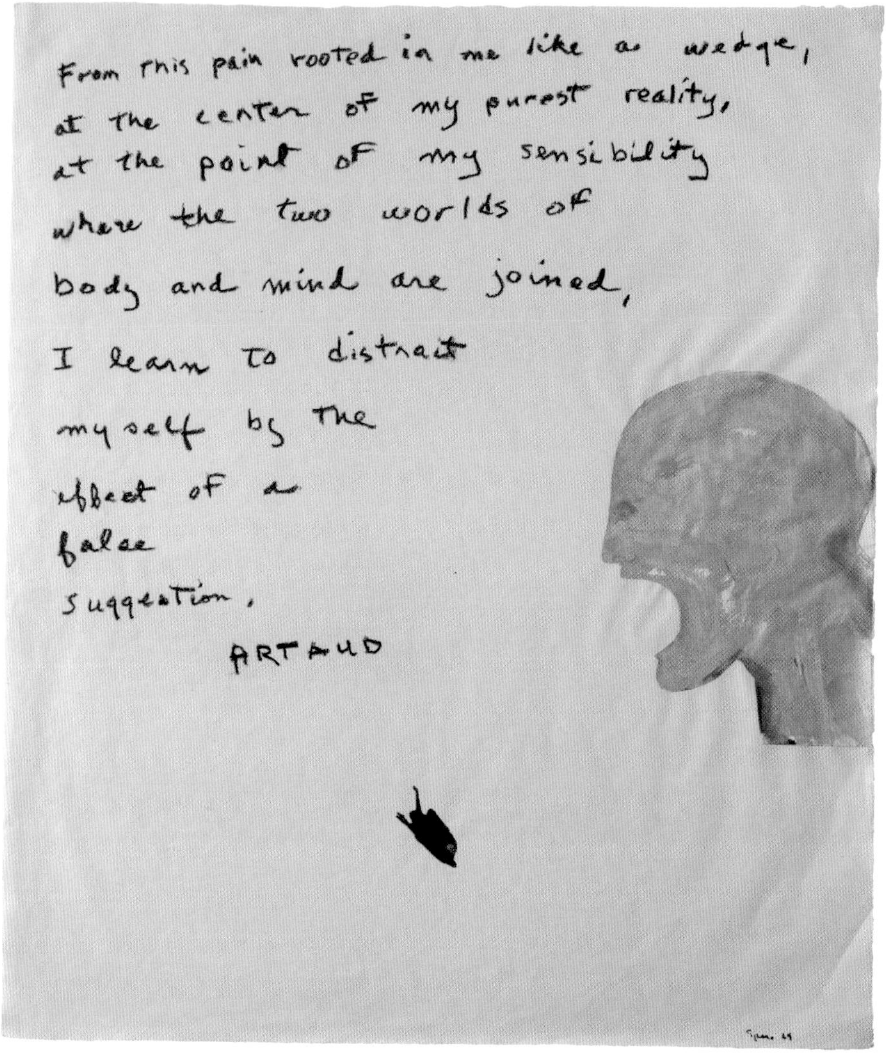

22
Artaud Painting – From this pain..., 1969
Gouache, ink and collage on paper,
63.5 × 52.7 cm (25 × 20 ¾ in.)

MACBA Collection. MACBA Foundation, Barcelona
Photo: FotoGasull

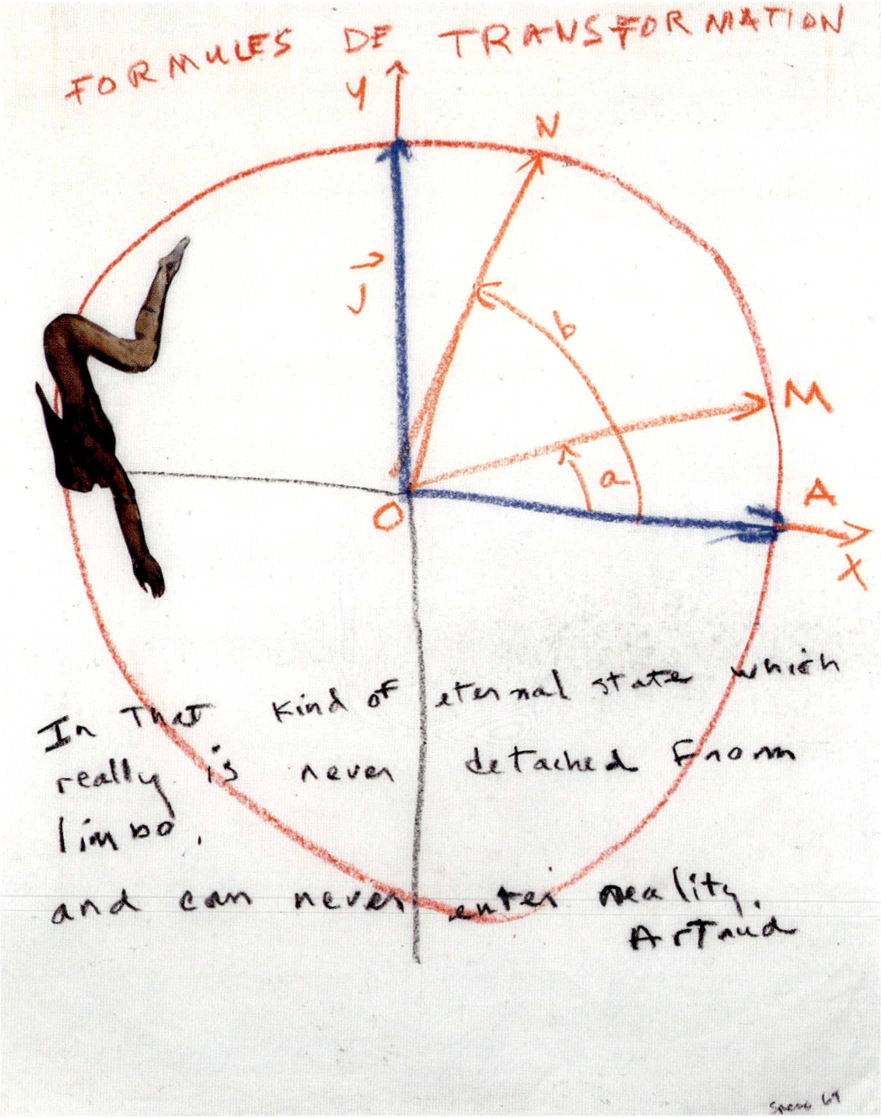

23
Artaud Painting – Formules de transformation, 1969
Oil stick, paint and collage on paper,
63.2 × 50.8 cm (24 ⅞ × 20 in.)

Vancouver Art Gallery. Gift of Keith Westergaard and Cordell Couillard
Photo: David Reynolds. Courtesy The Nancy Spero and Leon Golub
Foundation for the Arts

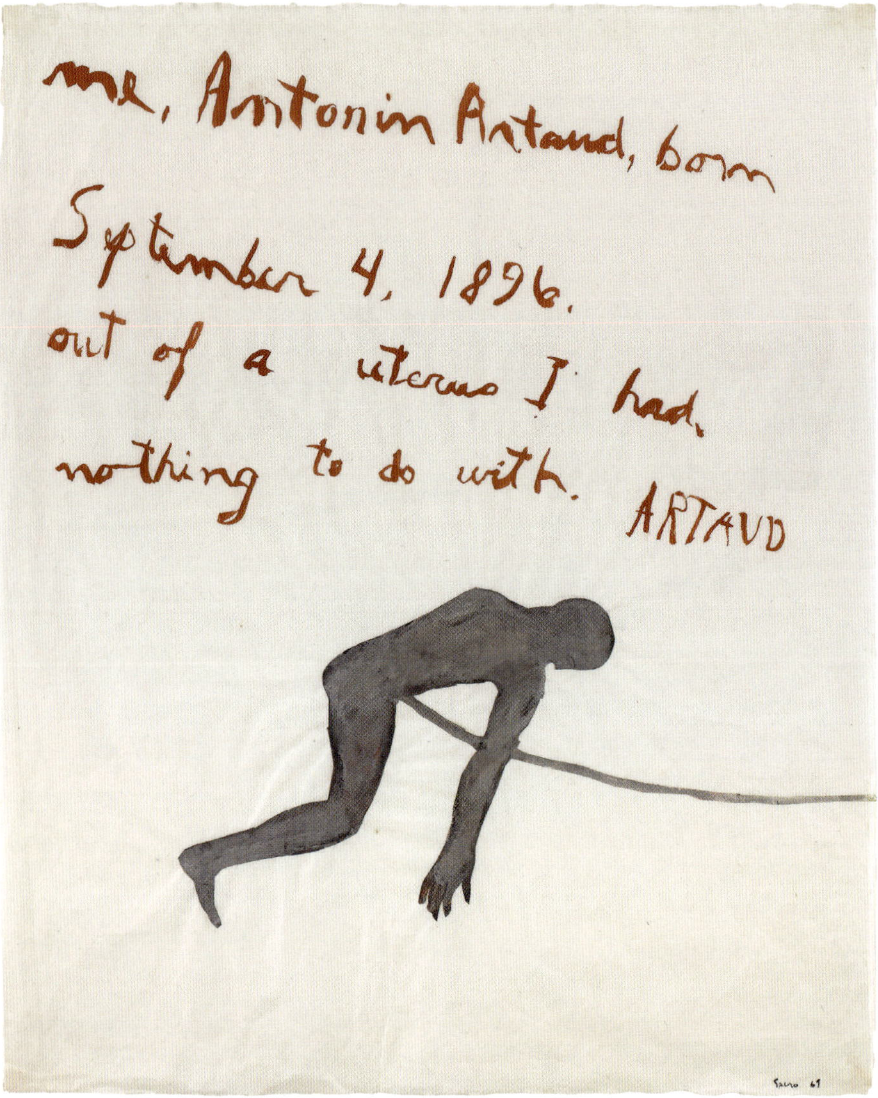

24
Me, Antonin Artaud, born September 4, 1896, out of a uterus I had nothing to do with, 1969
Gouache, ink, and collage of painted paper on paper, 63.6 × 50.2 cm (25 1⁄16 × 19 ¾ in.)

Centre Georges Pompidou, Paris. Donation de la Collection Florence et Daniel Guerlain, 2012
RMN-Grand Palais / André Morin / Dist. Photo SCALA, Florence

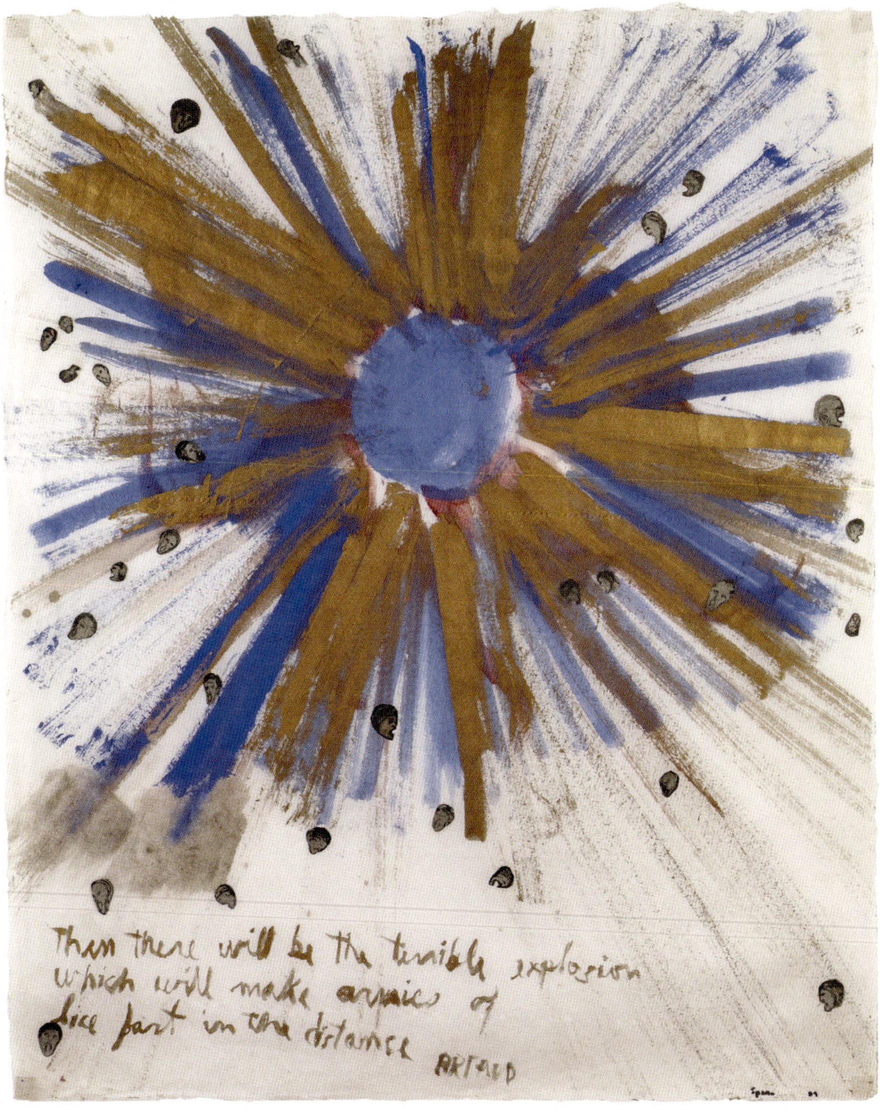

25
Artaud Painting – Then There Will Be..., 1969
Gouache, ink, and hand-painted collage on paper, 63.5 × 53.3 cm (25 × 21 in.)

Private Collection
Photo courtesy Galerie Lelong, New York

26
Artaud Painting – All writing is pigshit, 1969
Gouache on paper, 63.5 × 50.2 cm (25 × 19 ¾ in.)

Private Collection
Photo courtesy Galerie Lelong, New York

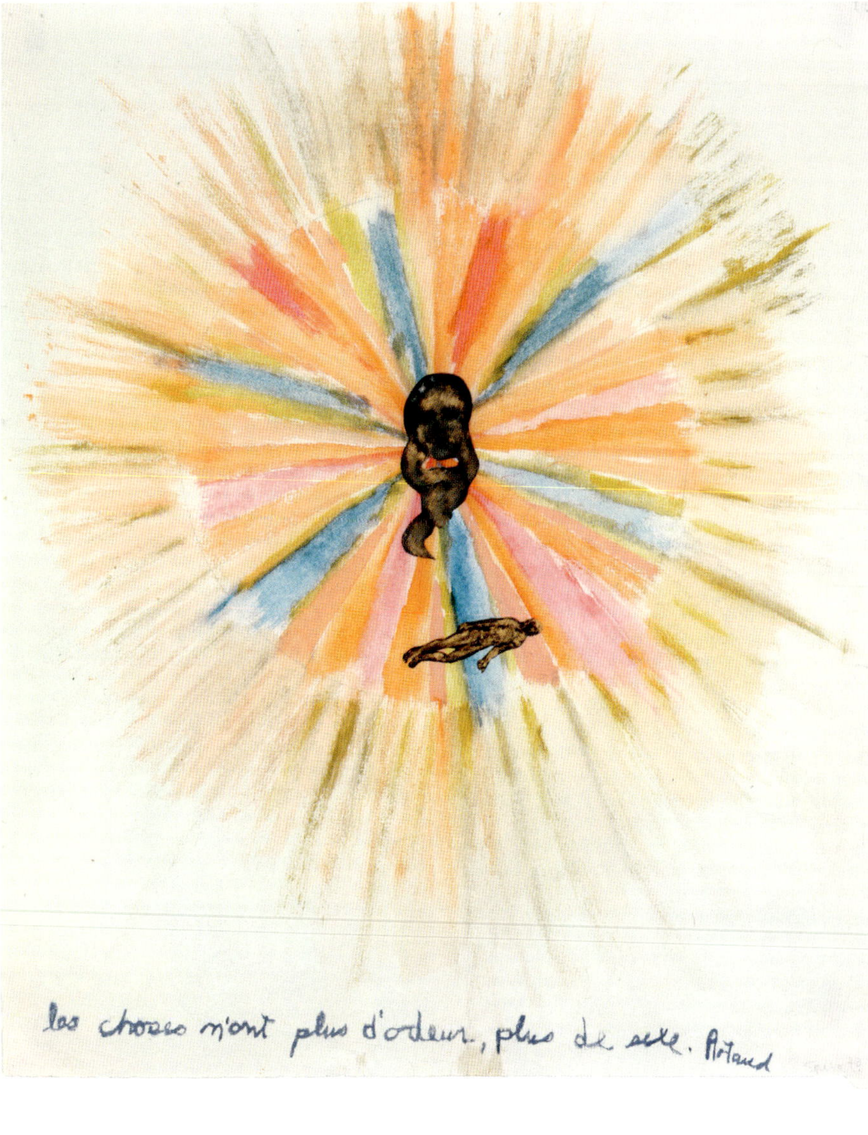

27
Artaud Painting – Les choses n'ont plus d'odeur..., 1970
Gouache and collage on paper,
63.5 × 52.1 cm (25 × 20 ½ in.)

The Stephen Golub Fine Arts Trust
Photo courtesy Galerie Lelong, New York

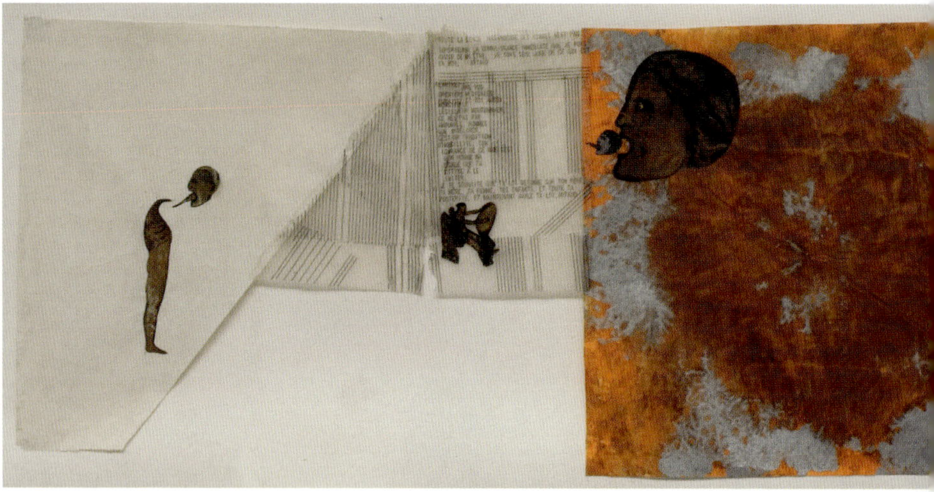

28
Codex Artaud I, 1971
Gouache and typewriter collage on paper,
58.4 × 243.8 cm (23 × 96 in.)

Fonds national d'art contemporain, Centre national des arts plastiques. On deposit at Centre Georges Pompidou, Paris
Photo courtesy Galerie Lelong, New York

29
Codex Artaud I, 1971 (detail)
Gouache and typewriter collage on paper,
58.4 × 243.8 cm (23 × 96 in.)

Fonds national d'art contemporain, Centre national des arts plastiques. On deposit at Centre Georges Pompidou, Paris
Photo courtesy Galerie Lelong, New York

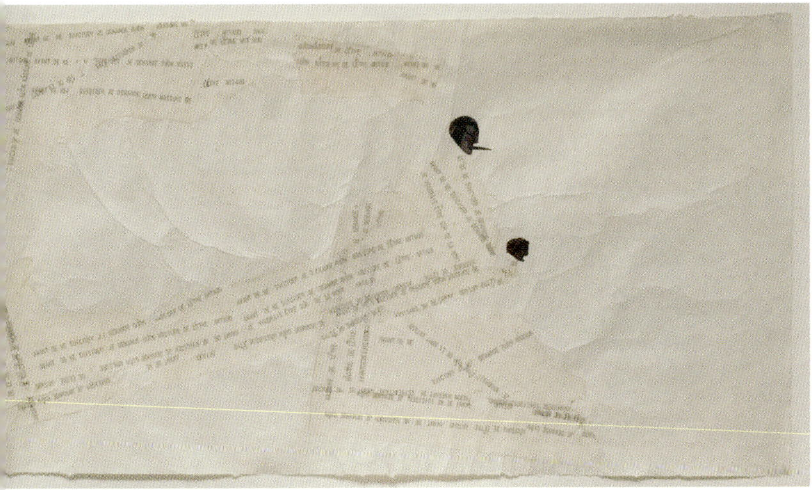

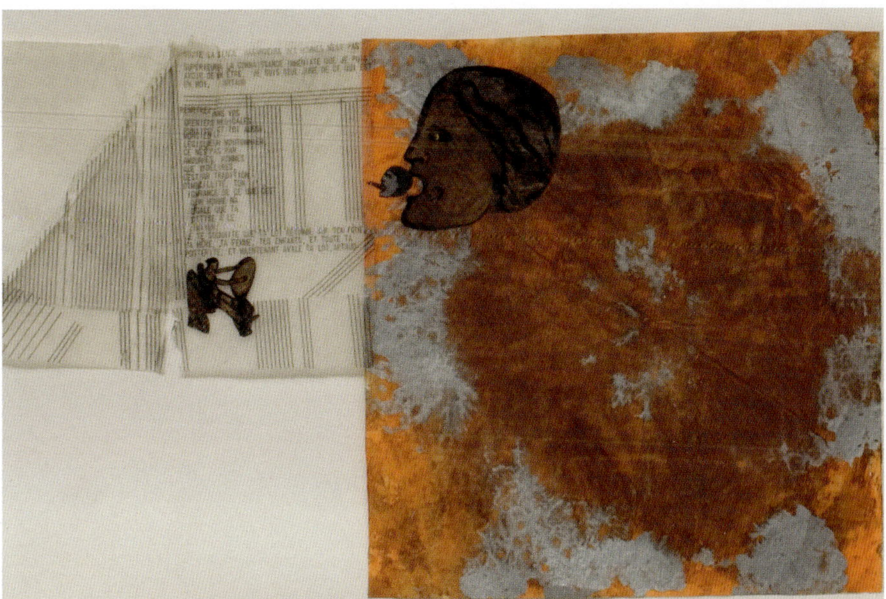

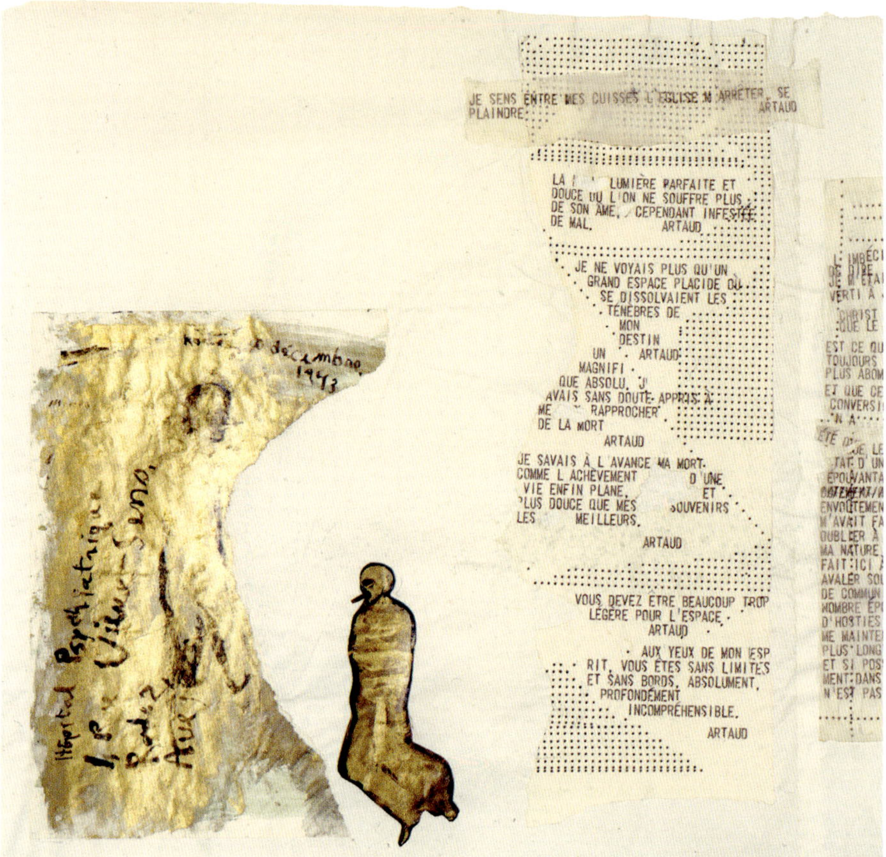

30
Codex Artaud VI, 1971 (detail)
Typewriting collage, cut-out painting, metallic paint and ink on paper, 52.1 × 316.2 cm (20 ½ × 124 ½ in.)

Museo Nacional Centro de Arte Reina Sofía, Madrid
Photo: David Reynolds. Courtesy The Nancy Spero and Leon Golub Foundation for the Arts

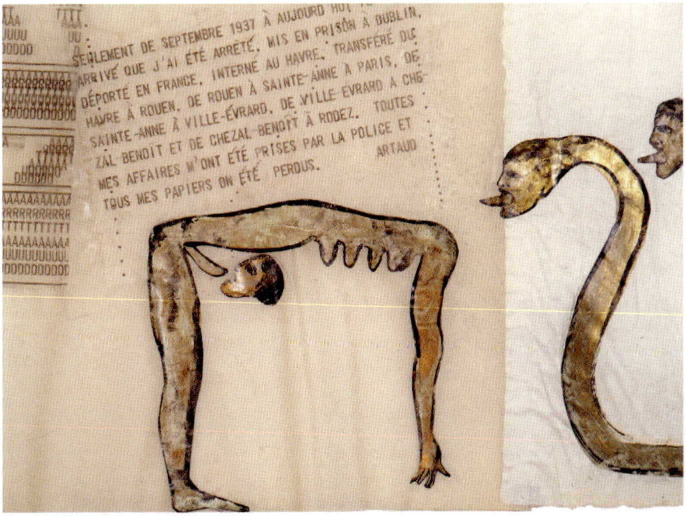

31
Codex Artaud VI, 1971 (detail)
Typescript, painting, and collage on paper,
52.1 × 316.2 cm (20 ½ × 124 ½ in.)

Museo Nacional Centro de Arte Reina Sofia, Madrid
Photo: David Reynolds. Courtesy The Nancy Spero and
Leon Golub Foundation for the Arts

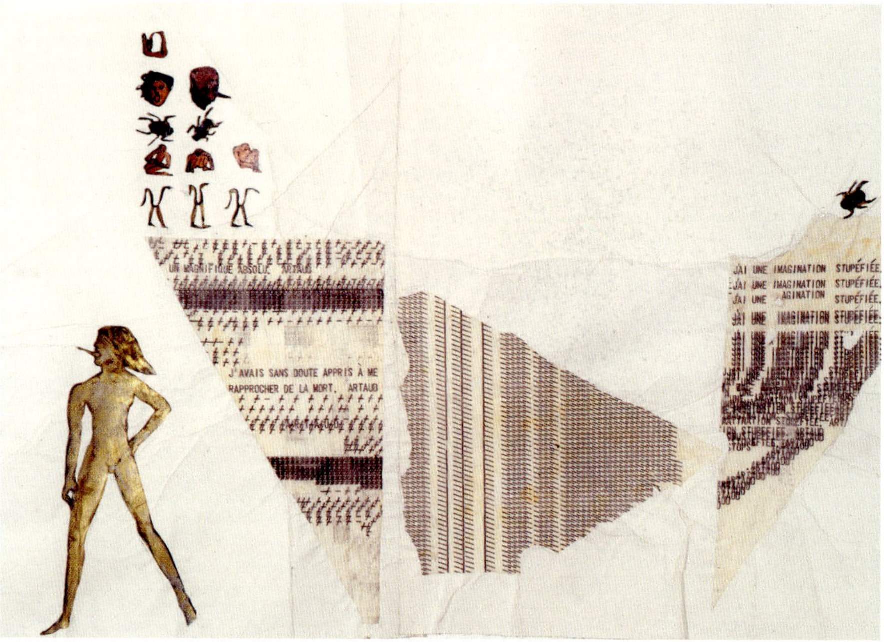

32
Codex Artaud VII, 1971 (detail)
Typescript, painting, and collage on paper,
52 × 381 cm (20 ½ × 150 in.)

Museo Nacional Centro de Arte Reina Sofia, Madrid
Photo: David Reynolds. Courtesy The Nancy Spero and
Leon Golub Foundation for the Arts

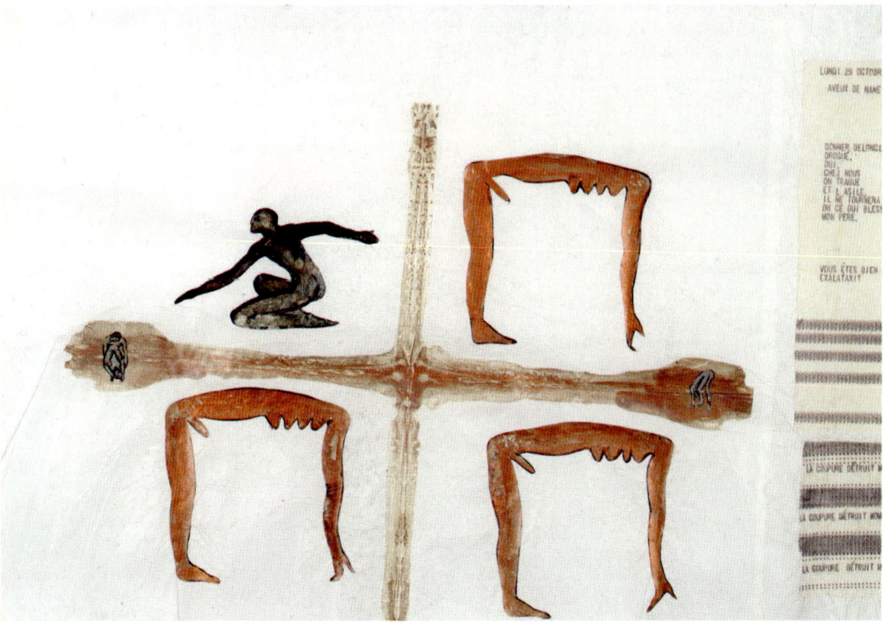

33
Codex Artaud XXV, 1971 (detail)
Typewriting collage, cut-out painting, collage on paper, 60.9 × 487.6 cm (24 × 192 in.)

Williams College Museum of Art, Williamstown, Massachusetts. Museum purchase, Kathryn Hurd Fund
Photo: David Reynolds. Courtesy The Nancy Spero and Leon Golub Foundation for the Arts

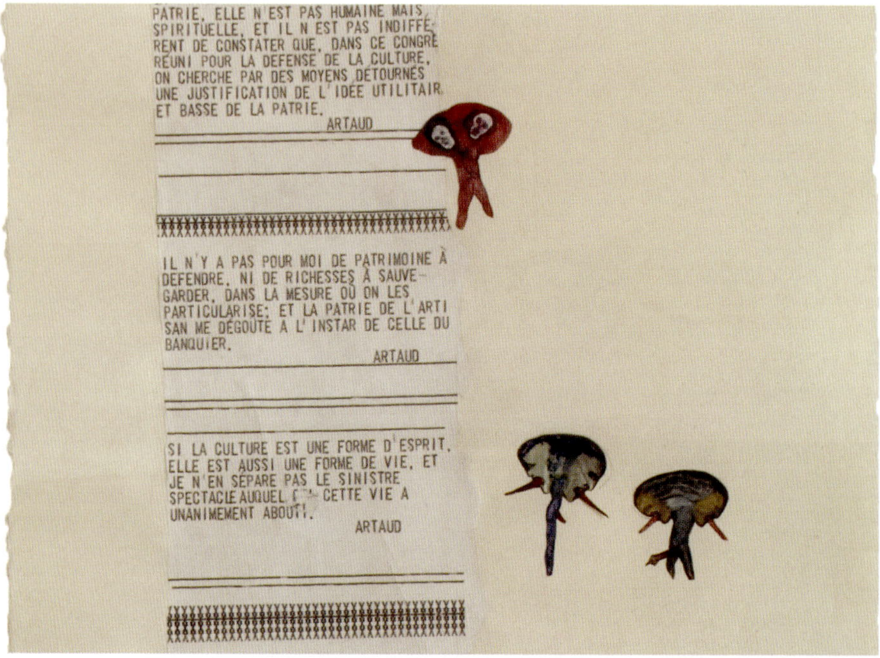

34
Codex Artaud XIII, 1972 (detail)
Typescript, gouache, and collage on paper,
113 × 44.5 cm (44 ½ × 17 ½ in.)

MACBA Collection. MACBA Foundation, Barcelona
Photo courtesy Galerie Lelong, New York

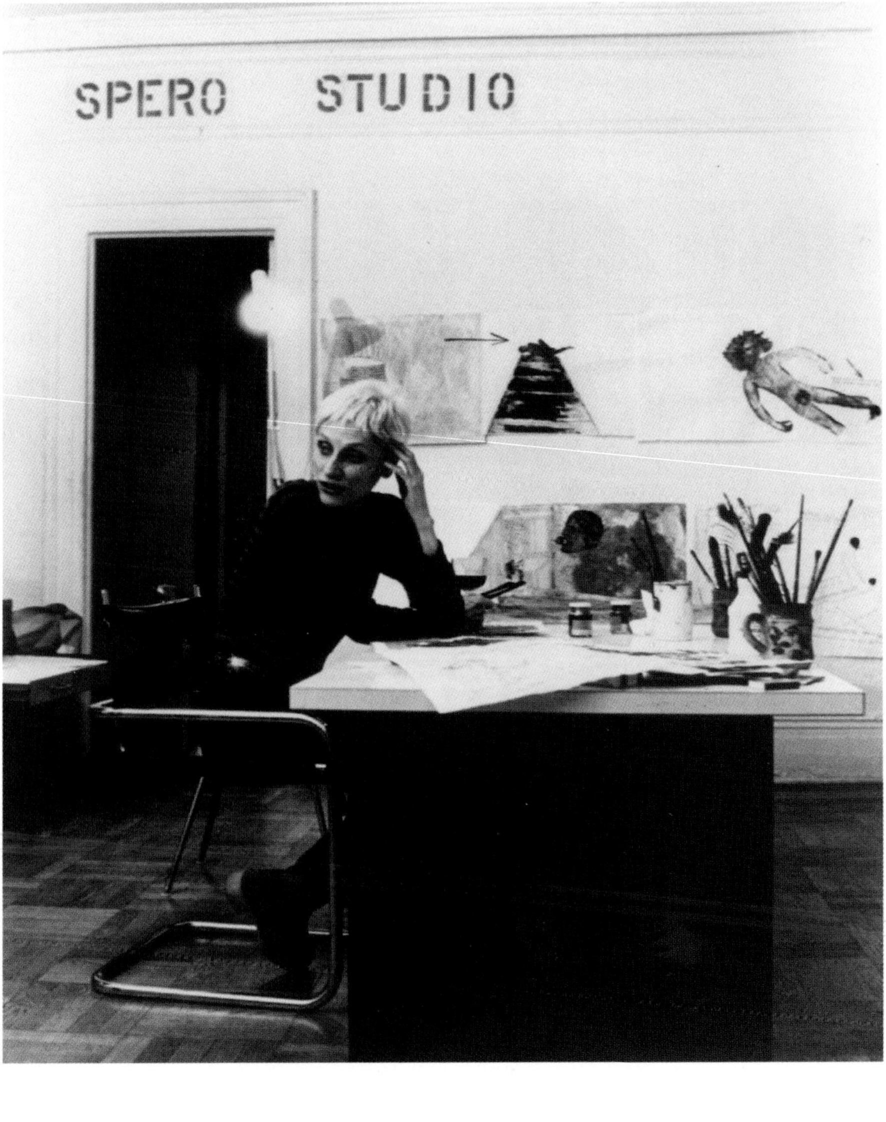

35
Nancy Spero in her 71st Street studio with *Codex Artaud* panels behind her on the wall, New York, 1973

Photo: Susan Weiley. Courtesy Galerie Lelong, New York

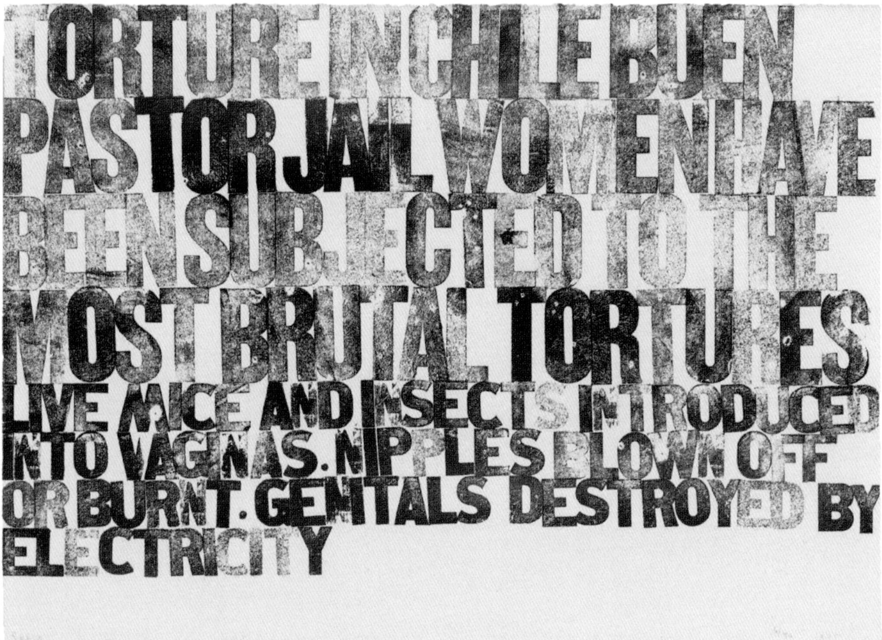

36
Torture in Chile, 1975
Silkprint, 57.2 × 76.8 cm (22 ½ × 30 ¼ in.)
Printed and published by A.I.R. Gallery
Edition 6/30

Whitney Museum of American Art, New York.
Purchase, with funds from the Print Committee
Digital image Whitney Museum of American Art /
Licensed by Scala

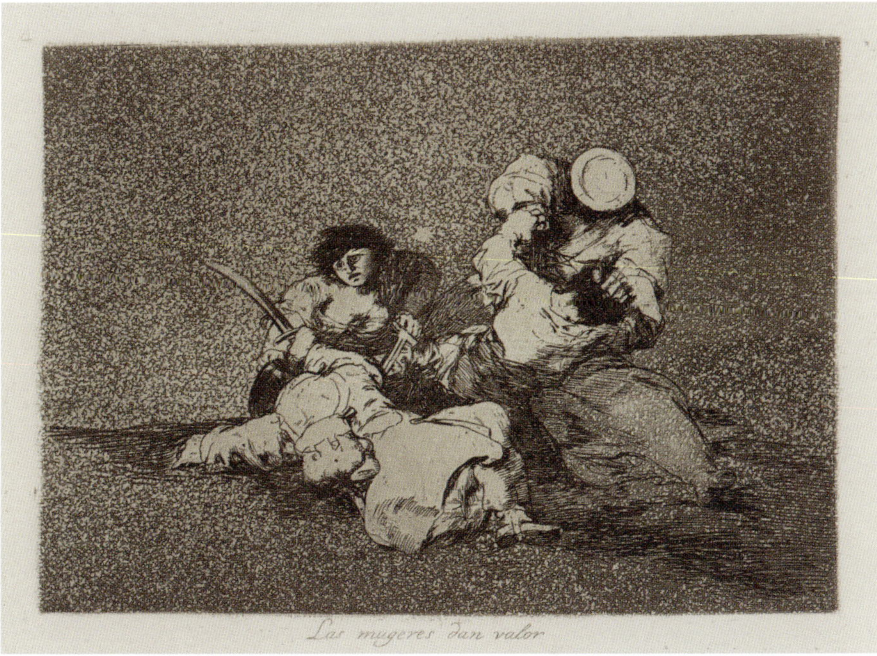

37
Francisco Goya (1746–1828)
Las mugeres dan valor (The Women Give Courage), pl. 4 from the series *Los desastres de la guerra* (The Disasters of War), 1810–20, published 1863
Etching, burnished aquatint, lavis drypoint, and burnisher on wove paper; platemark: 15.5 × 20.5 cm (6 1/8 × 8 1/16 in.)

Yale University Art Gallery. The Arthur Ross Collection

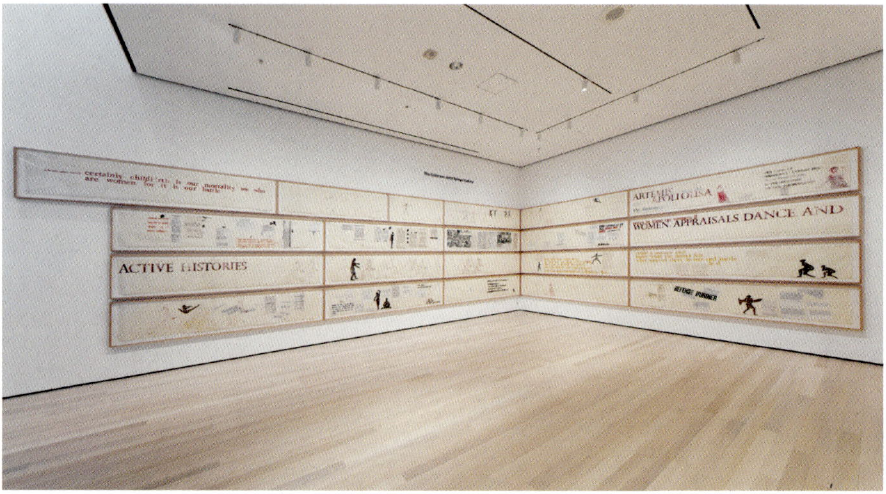

38 and (on following page, from top) 39, 40
Installation view of the gallery "Nancy Spero's Notes in Time" in the exhibition *Collection 1940s–1970s*, The Museum of Modern Art, New York, 25 January 2022 – 22 January 2023

Photo: Robert Gerhardt. Digital image, The Museum of Modern Art, New York/Scala, Florence

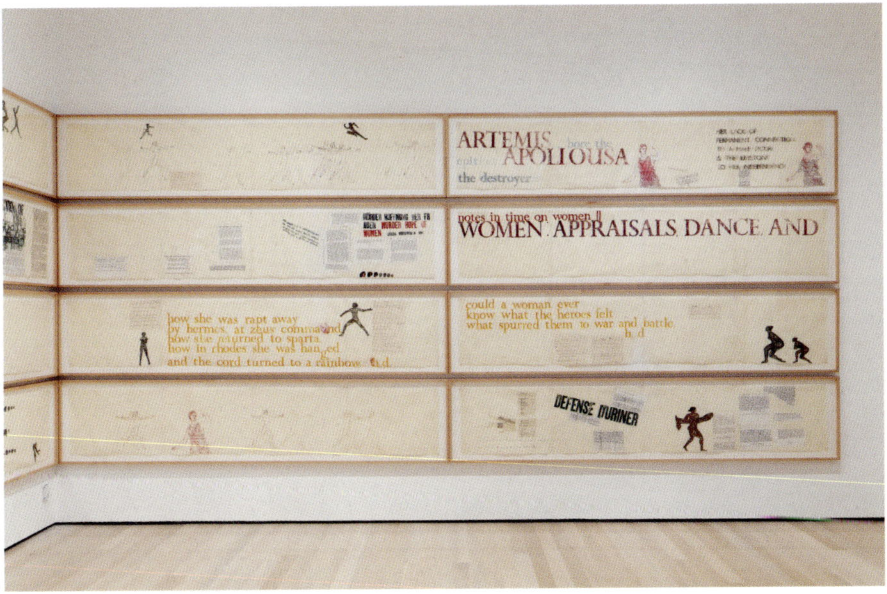

ARTEMIS
APOLLOUSA
the destroyer
notes in time on women II
WOMEN: APPRAISALS DANCE AND
how she was rapt away
by hermes, at zeus command
how she returned to sparta
how in rhodes she was hanged
and the cord turned to a rainbow h.d.
could a woman ever
know what the heroes felt
what spurred them to war and battle.
h.d
DEFENSE D'URINER

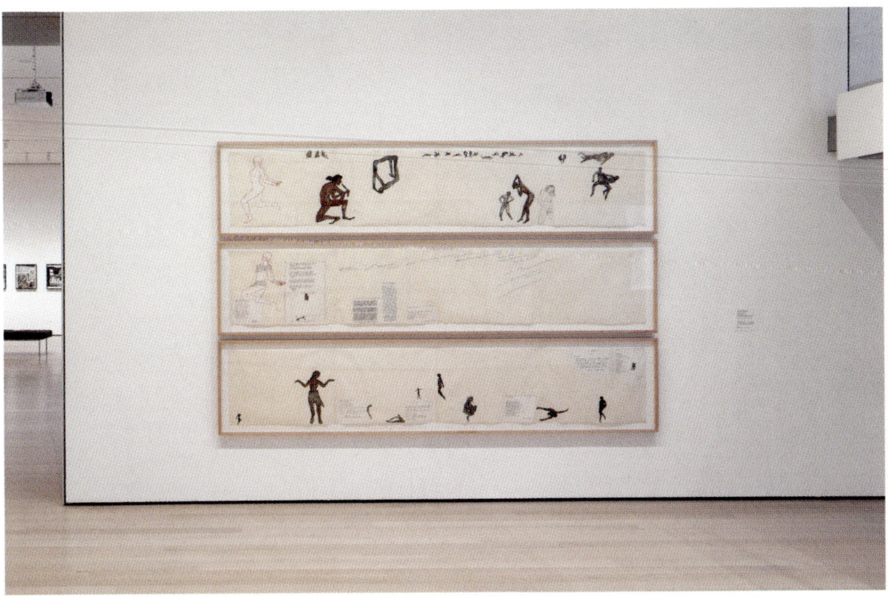

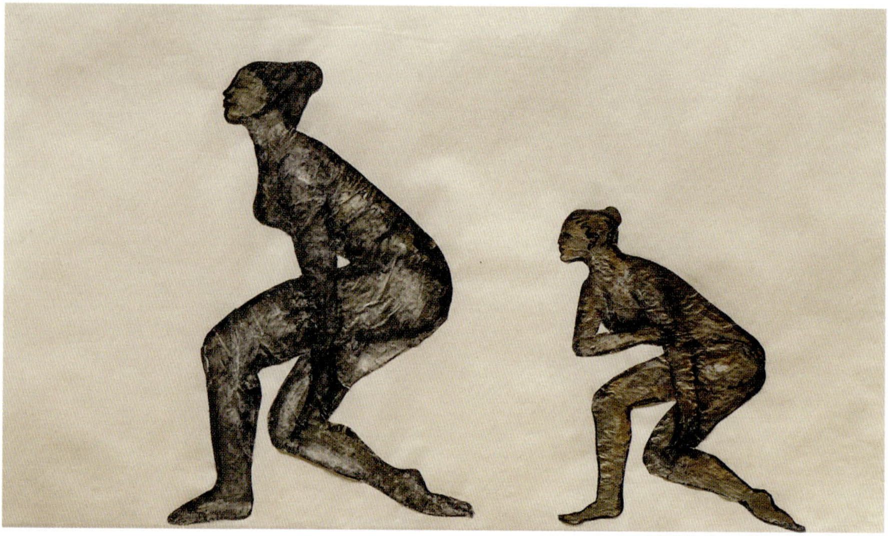

41
Notes in Time, 1979 (detail)
Cut-and-pasted painted paper, gouache, and pencil on joined sheets of paper, 24 panels, overall: 50.8 × 6400.8 cm (20 in. × 210 ft.)

The Museum of Modern Art, New York. Gift of Harriet and Rick Meyer
Photo courtesy Galerie Lelong, New York

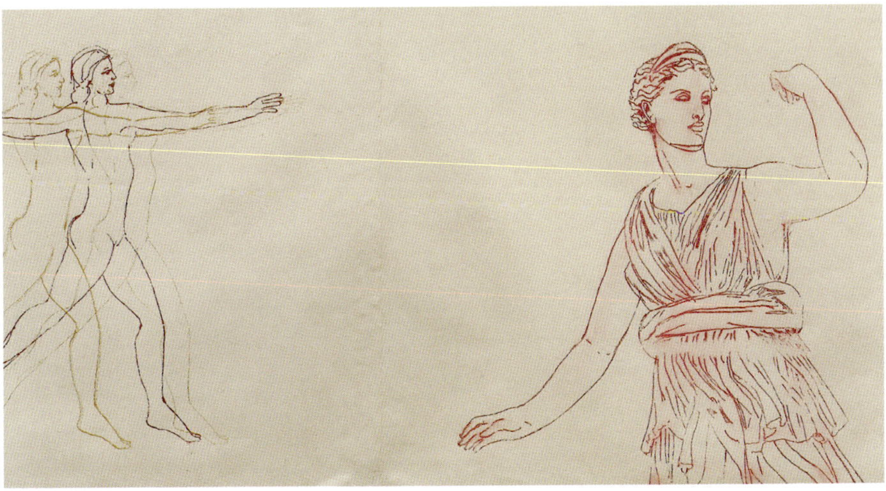

42
Notes in Time, 1979 (detail)
Cut-and-pasted painted paper, gouache, and pencil on joined sheets of paper, 24 panels
overall: 50.8 × 6400.8 cm (20 in. × 210 ft.)

The Museum of Modern Art, New York. Gift of Harriet and Rick Meyer
Photo courtesy Galerie Lelong, New York

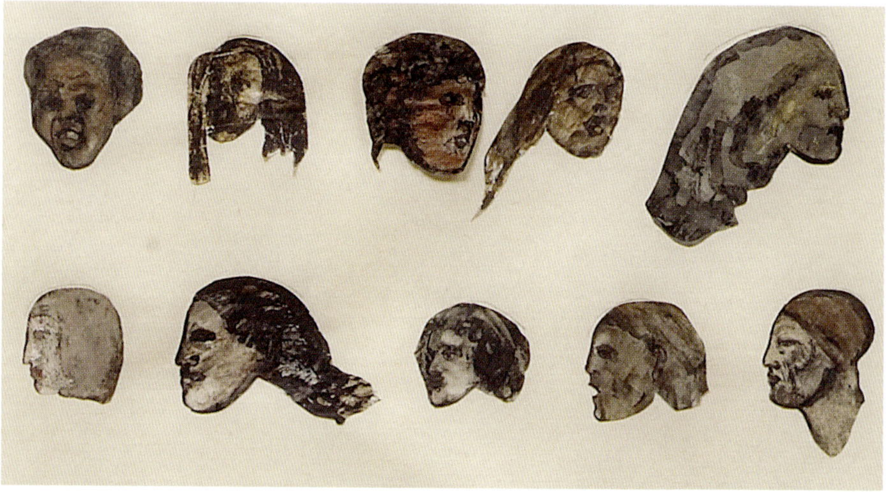

43
Notes in Time, 1979 (detail)
Cut-and-pasted painted paper, gouache,
and pencil on joined sheets of paper, 24 panels,
overall: 50.8 × 6400.8 cm (20 in. × 210 ft.)

The Museum of Modern Art, New York. Gift of Harriet and Rick Meyer
Photo courtesy Galerie Lelong, New York

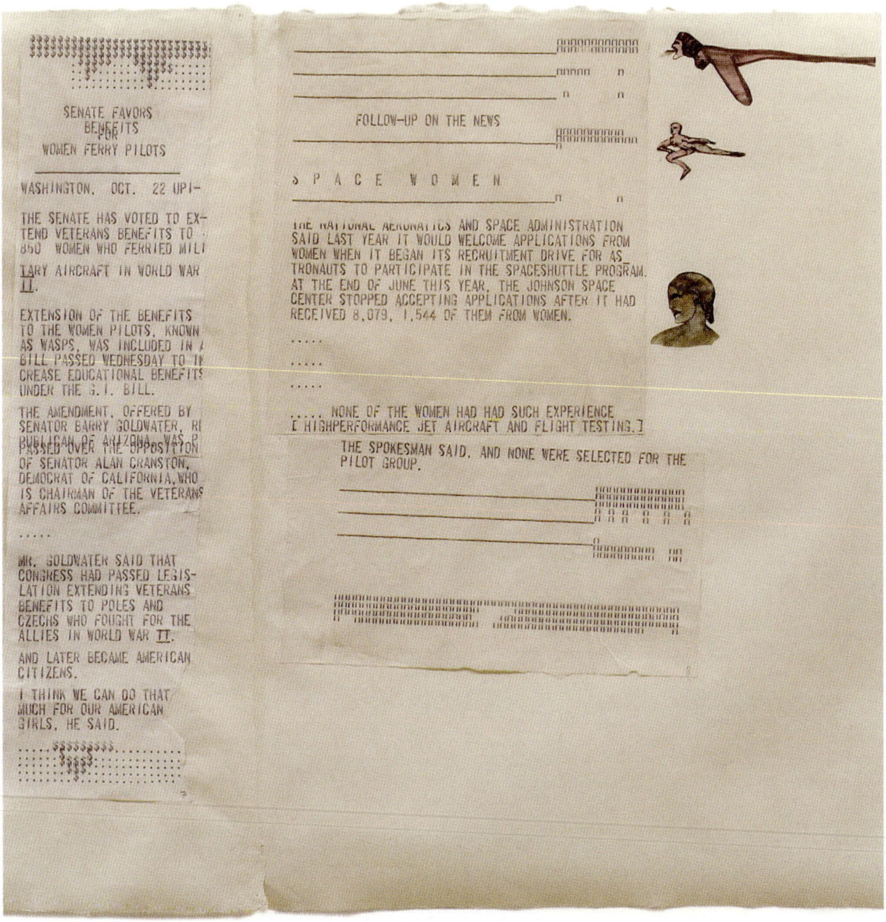

44
Notes in Time, 1979 (detail)
Cut-and-pasted painted paper, gouache, and pencil on joined sheets of paper, 24 panels, overall: 50.8 × 6400.8 cm (20 in. × 210 ft.)

The Museum of Modern Art, New York. Gift of Harriet and Rick Meyer
Photo courtesy Galerie Lelong, New York

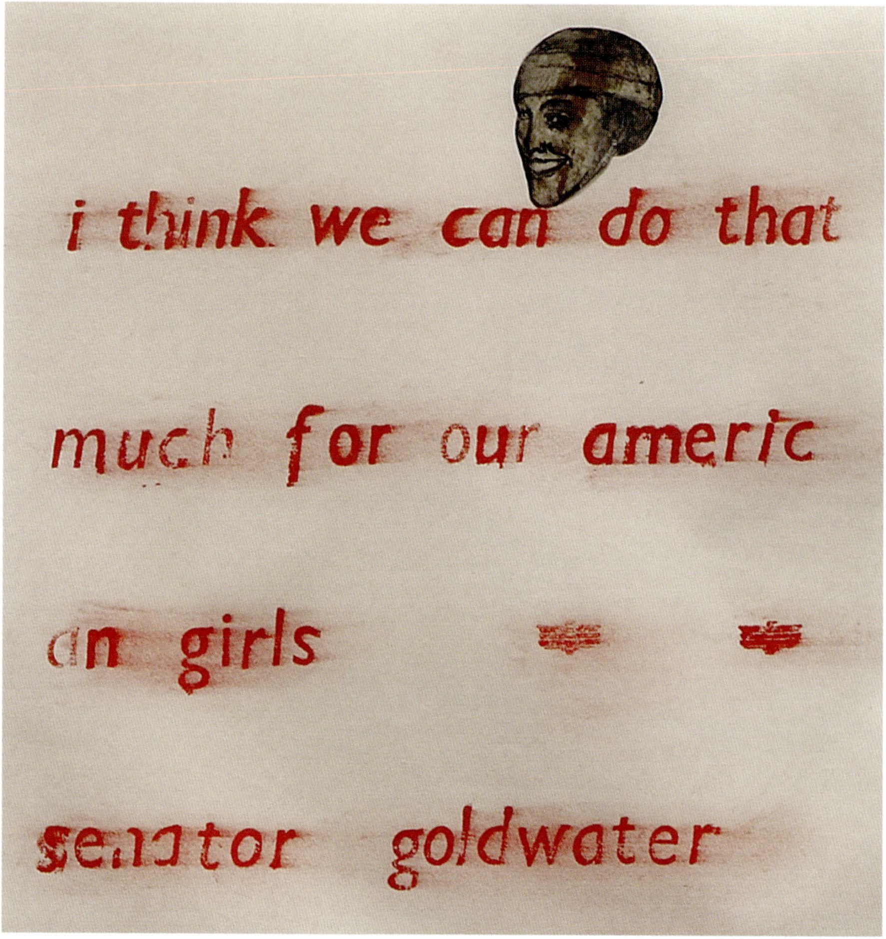

45
Notes in Time, 1979 (detail)
Cut-and-pasted painted paper, gouache,
and pencil on joined sheets of paper, 24 panels,
overall: 50.8 × 6400.8 cm (20 in. × 210 ft.)

The Museum of Modern Art, New York. Gift of Harriet and Rick Meyer
Photo courtesy Galerie Lelong, New York

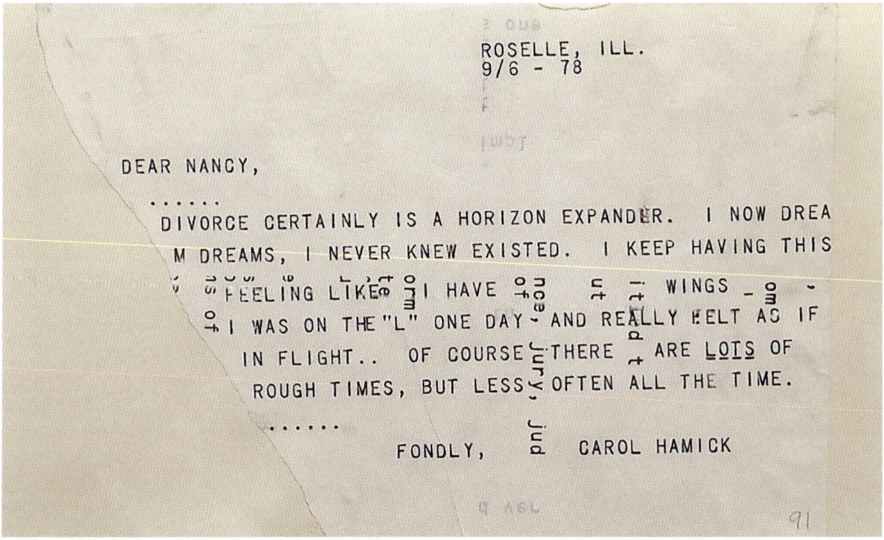
ROSELLE, ILL.
9/6 - 78

DEAR NANCY,

......
DIVORCE CERTAINLY IS A HORIZON EXPANDER. I NOW DREA
M DREAMS, I NEVER KNEW EXISTED. I KEEP HAVING THIS
FEELING LIKE I HAVE WINGS
I WAS ON THE "L" ONE DAY AND REALLY FELT AS IF
IN FLIGHT.. OF COURSE THERE ARE LOTS OF
ROUGH TIMES, BUT LESS OFTEN ALL THE TIME.
......
FONDLY, CAROL HAMICK

91

46
Notes in Time, 1979 (detail)
Cut-and-pasted painted paper, gouache,
and pencil on joined sheets of paper, 24 panels,
overall: 50.8 × 6400.8 cm (20 in. × 210 ft.)

The Museum of Modern Art, New York. Gift of Harriet and Rick Meyer
Photo courtesy Galerie Lelong, New York

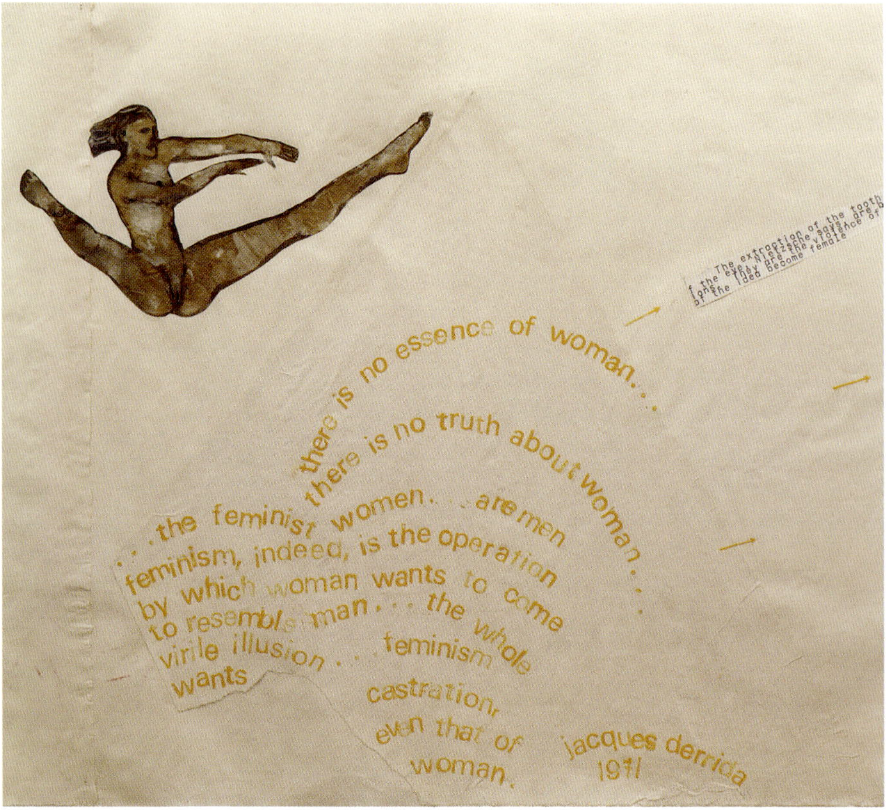

47
Notes in Time, 1979 (detail)
Cut-and-pasted painted paper, gouache, and pencil on joined sheets of paper, 24 panels, overall: 50.8 × 6400.8 cm (20 in. × 210 ft.)

The Museum of Modern Art, New York. Gift of Harriet and Rick Meyer
Photo courtesy Galerie Lelong, New York

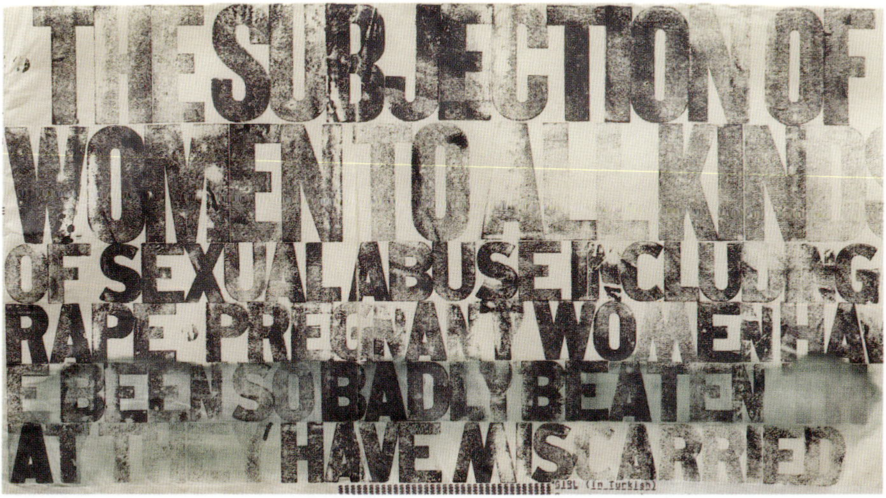

48
Notes in Time, 1979 (detail)
Cut-and-pasted painted paper, gouache, and pencil on joined sheets of paper, 24 panels, overall: 50.8 × 6400.8 cm (20 in. × 210 ft.)

The Museum of Modern Art, New York. Gift of Harriet and Rick Meyer
Photo courtesy Galerie Lelong, New York

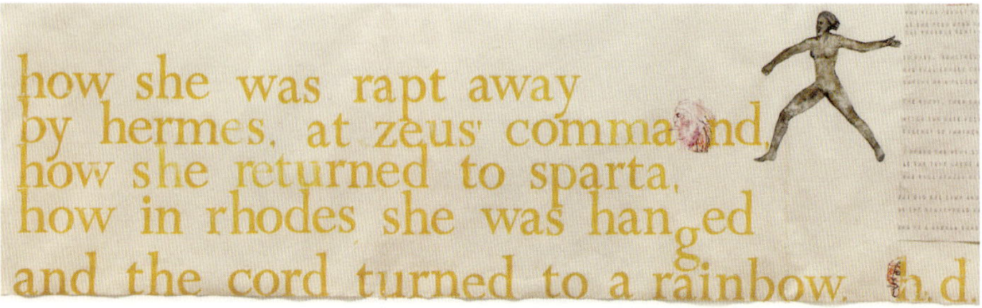

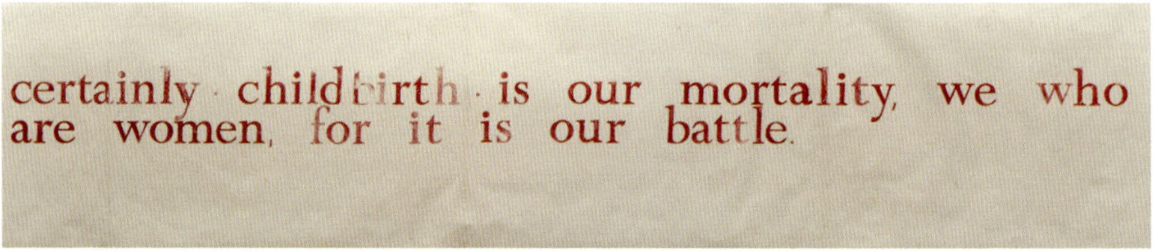

49, 50
Notes in Time, 1979 (detail)
Cut-and-pasted painted paper, gouache,
and pencil on joined sheets of paper, 24 panels,
overall: 50.8 × 6400.8 cm (20 in. × 210 ft.)

The Museum of Modern Art, New York. Gift of Harriet and Rick Meyer
Photo courtesy Galerie Lelong, New York

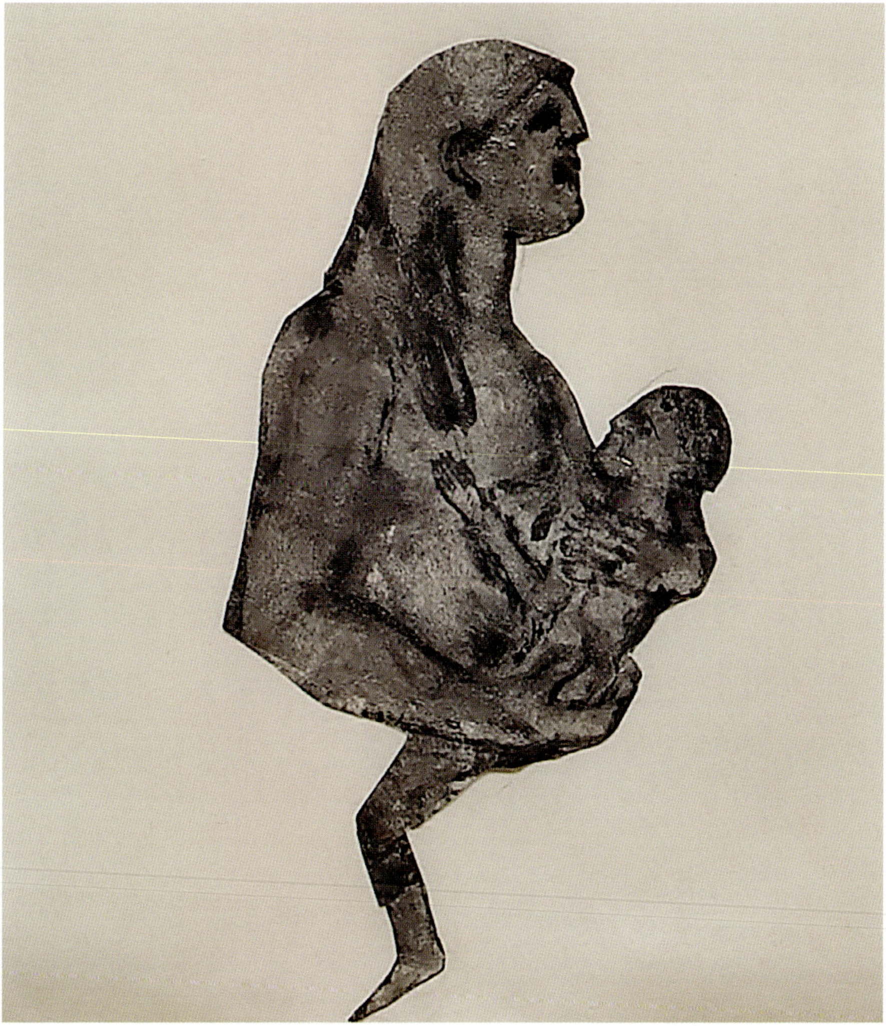

51
Notes in Time, 1979 (detail)
Cut-and-pasted painted paper, gouache,
and pencil on joined sheets of paper, 24 panels,
overall: 50.8 × 6400.8 cm (20 in. × 210 ft.)

The Museum of Modern Art, New York. Gift of Harriet and Rick Meyer
Photo courtesy Galerie Lelong, New York

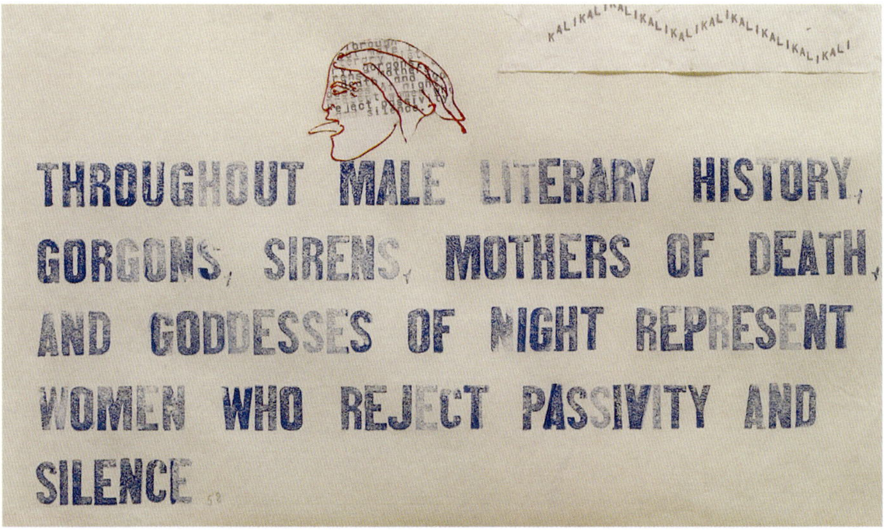

52
Notes in Time, 1979 (detail)
Cut-and-pasted painted paper, gouache,
and pencil on joined sheets of paper, 24 panels,
overall: 50.8 × 6400.8 cm (20 in. × 210 ft.)

The Museum of Modern Art, New York. Gift of Harriet and Rick Meyer
Photo courtesy Galerie Lelong, New York

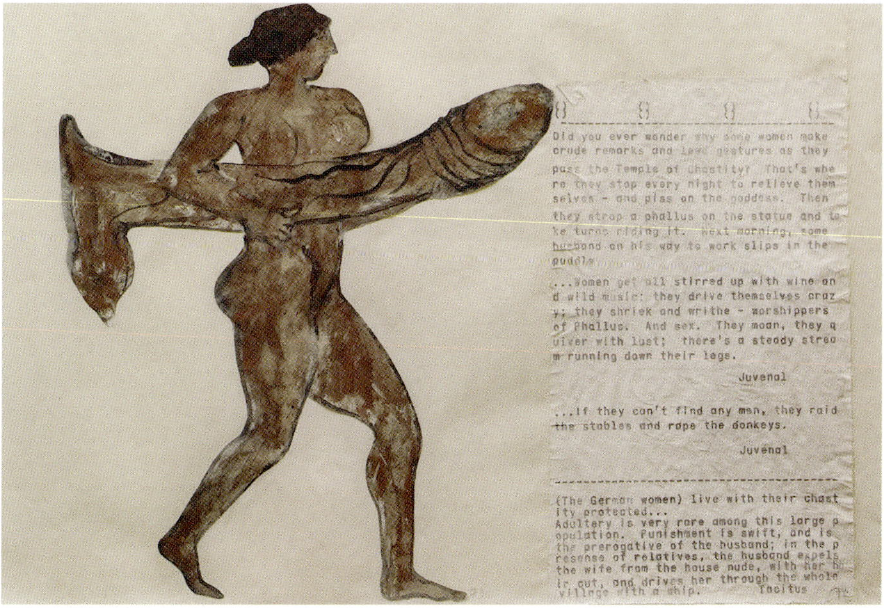

53
Notes in Time, 1979 (detail)
Cut-and-pasted painted paper, gouache, and pencil on joined sheets of paper, 24 panels, overall: 50.8 × 6400.8 cm (20 in. × 210 ft.)

The Museum of Modern Art, New York. Gift of Harriet and Rick Meyer
Photo courtesy Galerie Lelong, New York

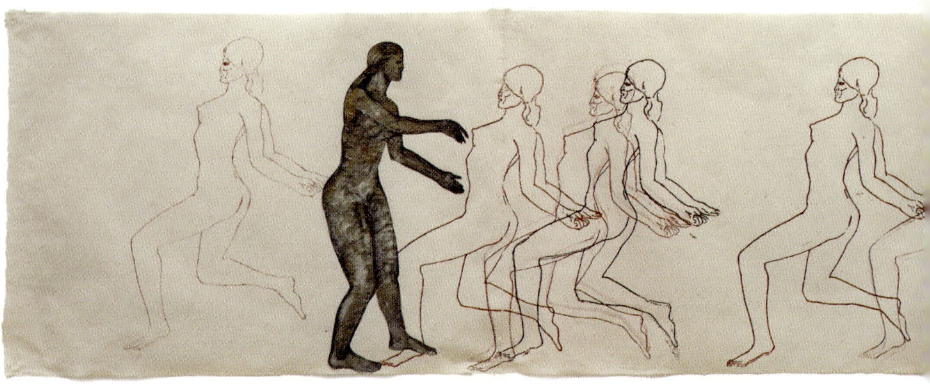

54
Notes in Time, 1979 (detail)
Cut-and-pasted painted paper, gouache,
and pencil on joined sheets of paper, 24 panels,
overall: 50.8 × 6400.8 cm (20 in. × 210 ft.)

The Museum of Modern Art, New York. Gift of Harriet and Rick Meyer
Photo courtesy Galerie Lelong, New York

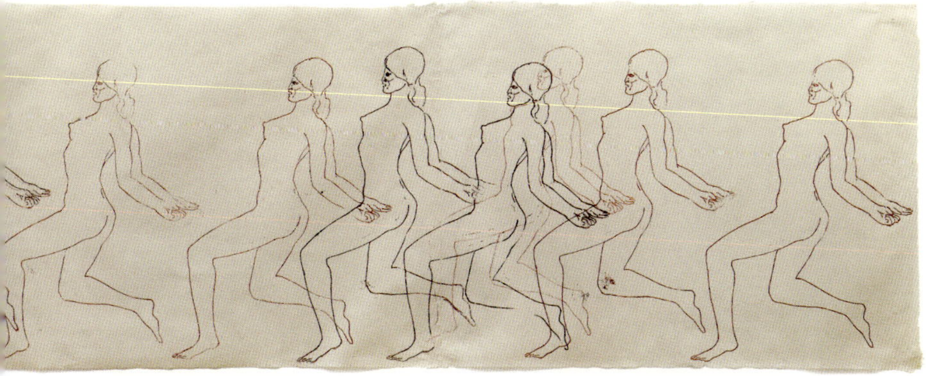

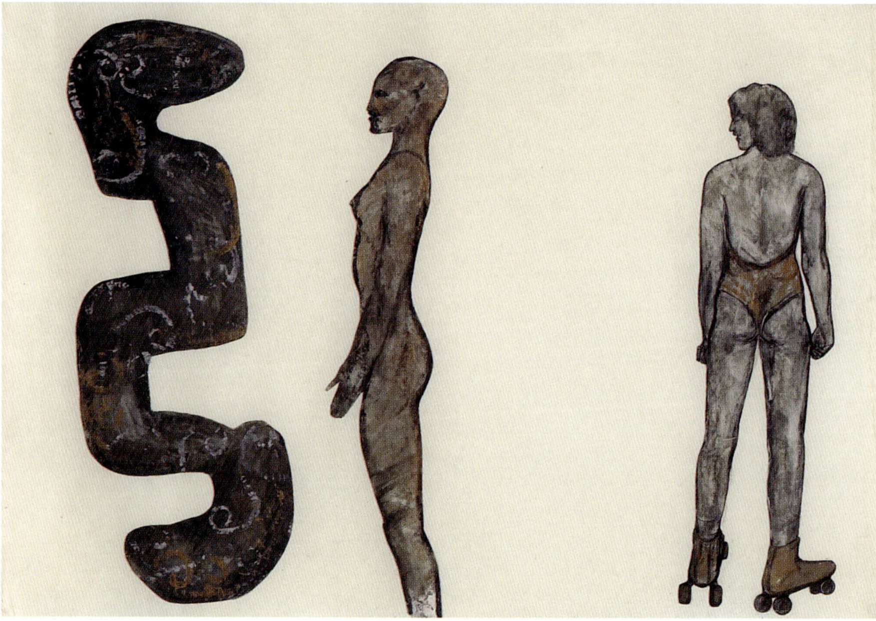

55
The First Language, 1981 (detail)
Handprinting, printed and painted collage on paper, 22 panels, overall: 50.8 × 5791.2 cm (20 in. × 190 ft.)

National Gallery of Canada, Ottawa. Purchased 2003
Photo: NGC

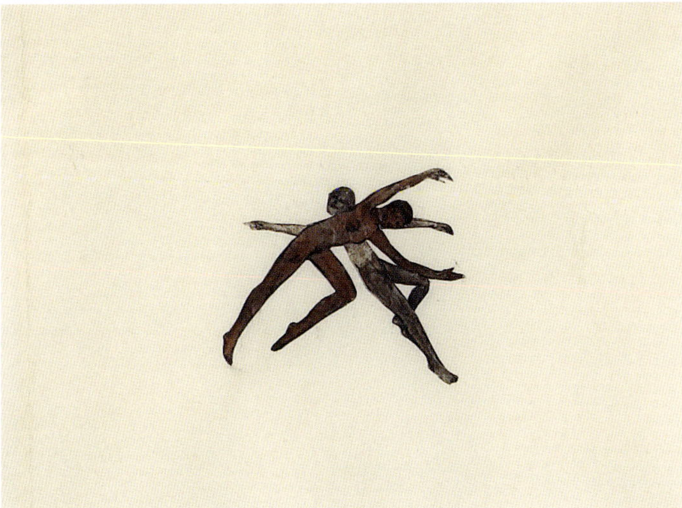

56
The First Language, 1981 (detail)
Handprinting, printed and painted collage on paper, 22 panels, overall: 50.8 × 5791.2 cm (20 in. × 190 ft.)

National Gallery of Canada, Ottawa. Purchased 2003
Photo: NGC

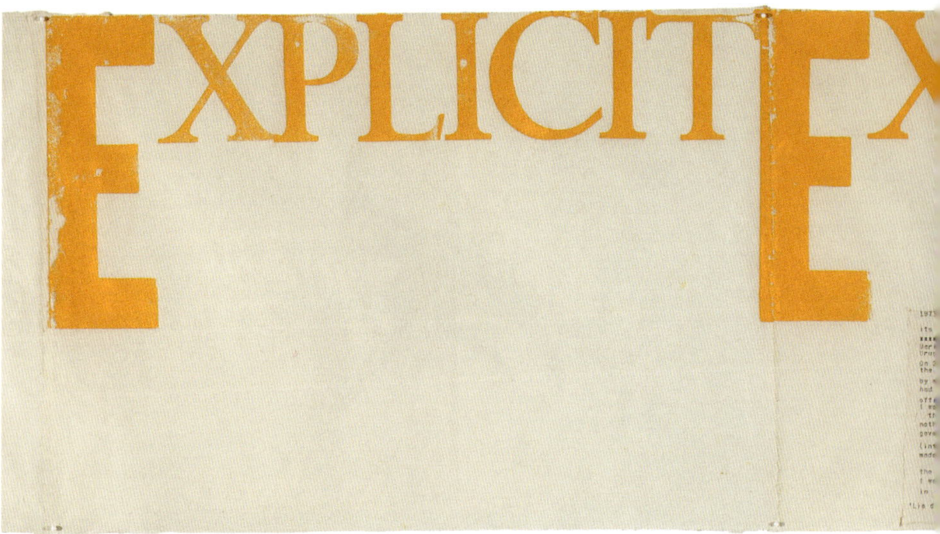

57
Torture of Women, 1976 (detail)
Gouache, typewritten texts, collage,
and hand-printing on laid paper, 14 panels,
overall: 50.8 × 3,810 cm (20 in. × 125 ft.)

National Gallery of Canada, Ottawa. Purchased 1993
Photo: NGC

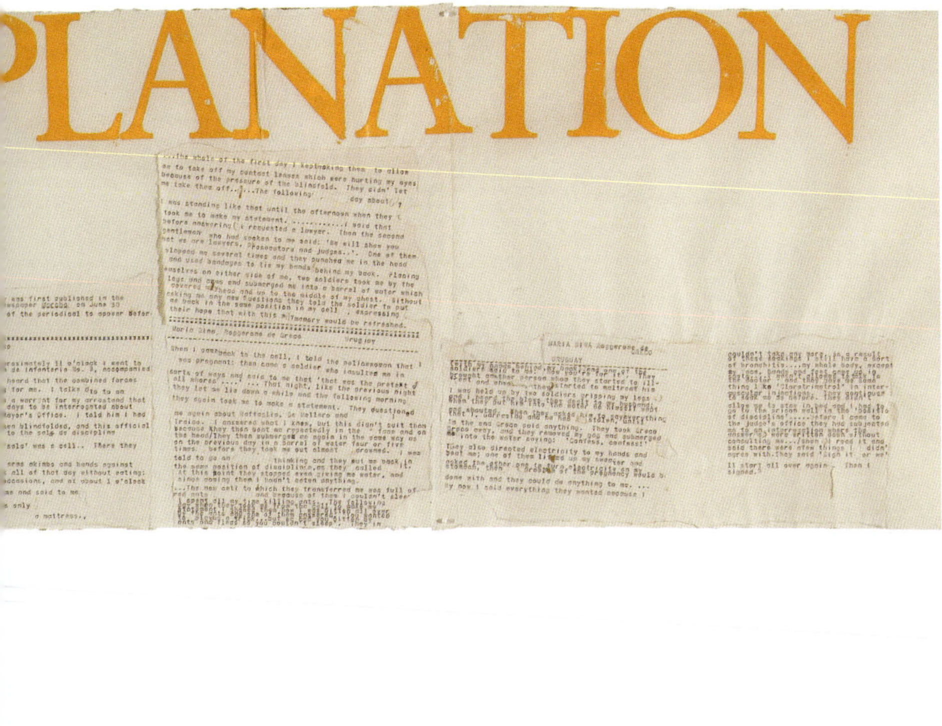
PLANATION
was first published in the
newspaper on June 30
of the periodical to appear befor
roximately 11 o'clock I went to
de Infanteria No. 3, accompanied
heard that the combined forces
for me.
a warrant for my arrest and that
days to be interrogated about
Mayor's Office. I told him I had
been blindfolded, and this official
to the sola de disciplina
sola' was a cell.. There they
arms akimbo and hands against
all of that day without eating:
occasions, and at about 1 o'clock
me and said to me
s only
a mattress..
...The whole of the first day I kept asking them to allow
me to take off my contact lenses which were hurting my eyes
because of the pressure of the blindfold. They didn't let
me take them off.......The following day about
I was standing like that until the afternoon when they
took me to make my statement. ....I said that
before answering I requested a lawyer. Then the second
gentleman who had spoken to me said: 'We will show you
that we are lawyers, prosecutors and judges..'. One of them
slapped me several times and they punched me in the head
and used bandages to tie my hands behind my back. Placing
themselves on either side of me, two soldiers took me by the
legs and arms and submerged me into a barrel of water which
covered my head and up to the middle of my chest. Without
asking me any new questions they told the soldier to put
me back in the same position in my cell, expressing
their hope that with this my memory would be refreshed.
Maria Dina, Reggerone de Greco Uruguay
When I came back to the cell, I told the policewoman that I
was pregnant: then came a soldier who insulted me in
all sorts of ways and said to me that 'that was the pretext of
all whores ....' ... That night, like the previous night
they let me lie down a while and the following morning
they again took me to make a statement. They questioned
me again about
Iraica. I answered what I knew, but this didn't suit them
because they then beat me repeatedly in the face and on
the head/They then submerged me again in the same way as
on the previous day in a barrel of water four or five
times before they took me out almost drowned. I was
told to go on thinking and they put me back in
the same position of discipline, as they called it.
At this point they stopped even giving me water, and
since coming there I hadn't eaten anything.
...The new cell to which they transferred me was full of
red ants and because of them I couldn't sleep
MARIA DINA Reggerone de GRECO
URUGUAY
I was held up by two soldiers gripping my legs
In the end Greco said anything. They took Greco
into the water saying: 'Confess, confess!'
They also directed electricity to my hands and
beat me; one of them lifted up my sweater and
done with and they could do anything to me. ...
By now I said everything they wanted because I
of bronchitis....my whole body, except
thing like 'Clorotrimetrol' in inter-
of discipline'.....Before I came to
the judge's office they had subjected
consulting me...when I read it and
said there were a few things I didn't
agree with. They said 'Sign it or we'
ll start all over again.' Then I
signed."

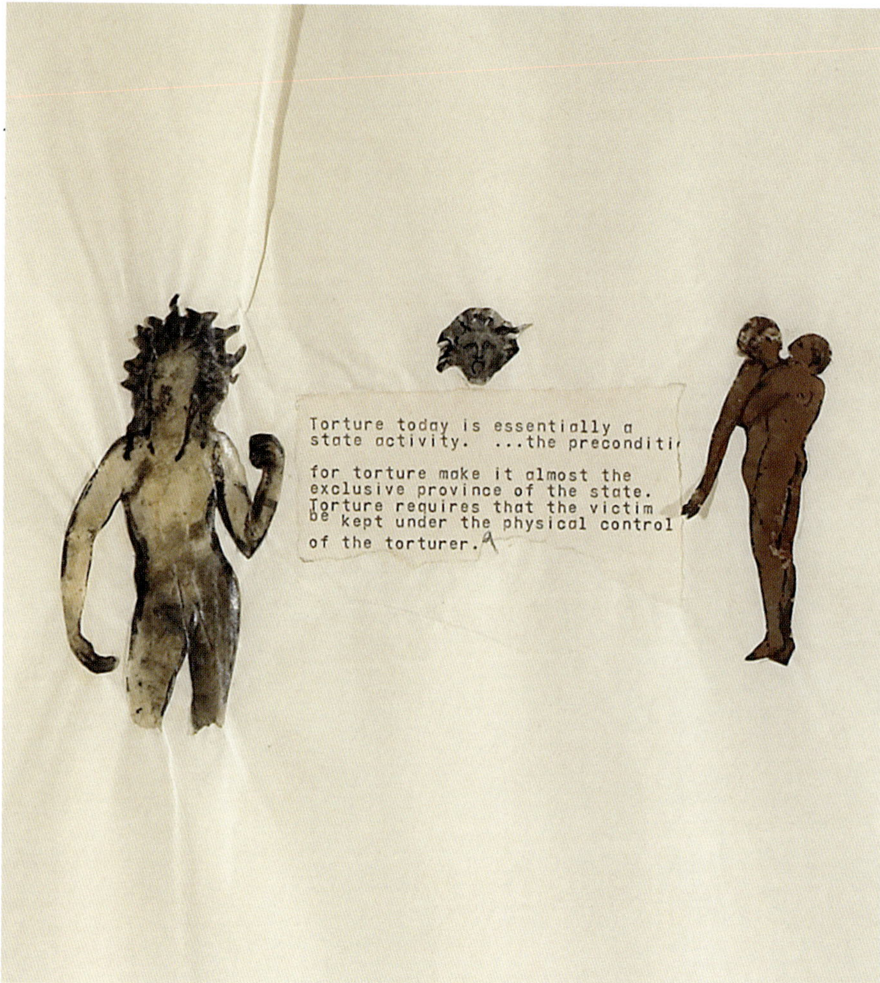

58
Torture of Women, 1976 (detail)
Gouache, typewritten texts, collage,
and hand-printing on laid paper, 14 panels,
overall: 50.8 × 3,810 cm (20 in. × 125 ft.)

National Gallery of Canada, Ottawa. Purchased 1993
Photo: NGC

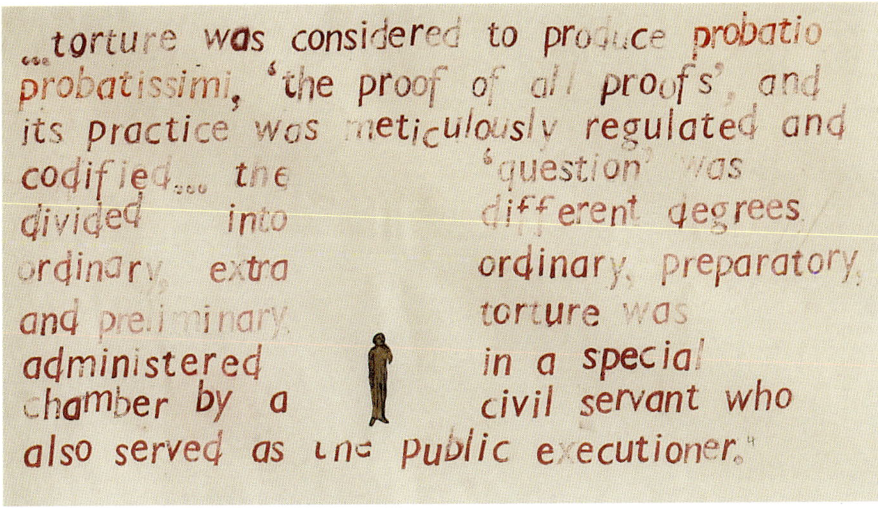

59
Torture of Women, 1976 (detail)
Gouache, typewritten texts, collage,
and hand-printing on laid paper, 14 panels,
overall: 50.8 × 3,810 cm (20 in. × 125 ft.)

National Gallery of Canada, Ottawa. Purchased 1993
Photo: NGC

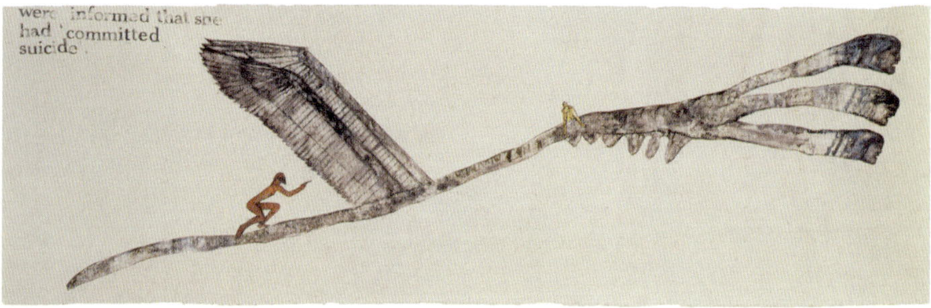

60
Torture of Women, 1976 (detail)
Gouache, typewritten texts, collage,
and hand-printing on laid paper, 14 panels,
overall: 50.8 × 3,810 cm (20 in. × 125 ft.)

National Gallery of Canada, Ottawa. Purchased 1993
Photo courtesy Galerie Lelong, New York

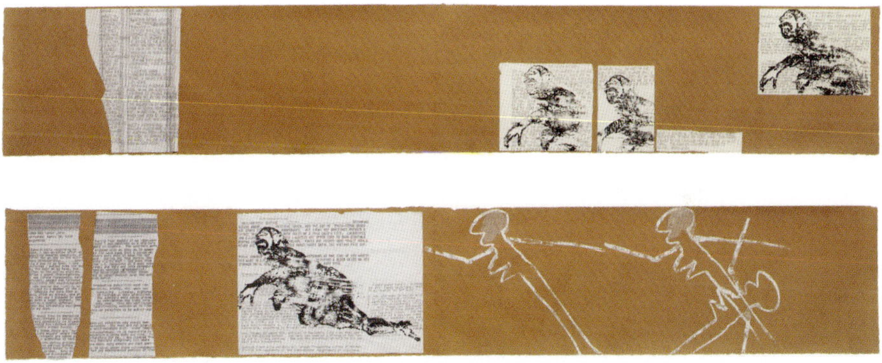

61
Torture of Women III, 1981
Handprinting and collage on paper, two parts,
each: 33.7 × 201.3 cm (13 ¼ × 79 ¼ in.)

Hirshhorn Museum and Sculpture Garden,
Smithsonian Institution, Washington, D.C.
Holenia Trust Fund, in memory of Joseph H.
Hirshhorn, 2009
Photo courtesy Galerie Lelong, New York

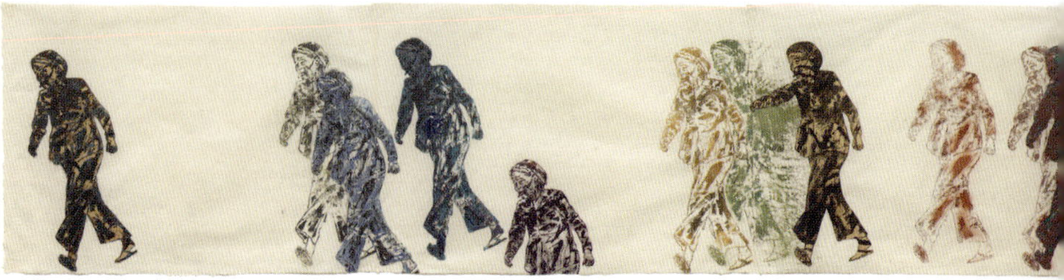

62
Vietnamese Women, 1985
Handprinting and printed
collage on paper, two parts, each:
50.8 × 213.4 cm (20 × 84 in.)

Private Collection
Photo courtesy Galerie Lelong, New York

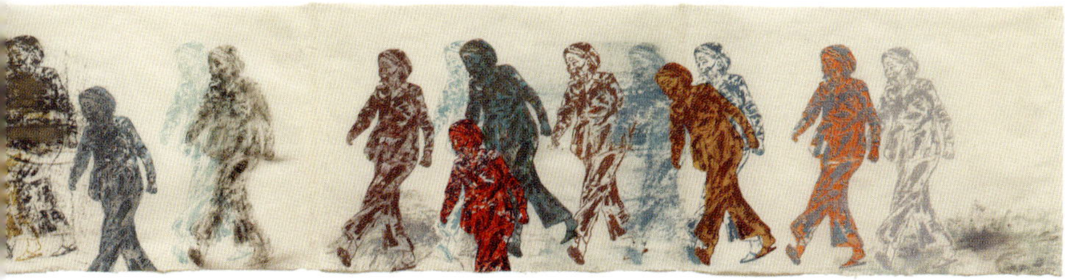

63
Vietnamese Women, 1985 (detail)
Handprinting and printed collage on paper, two parts, each: 50.8 × 213.4 cm (20 × 84 in.)

Private Collection
Photo courtesy Galerie Lelong, New York

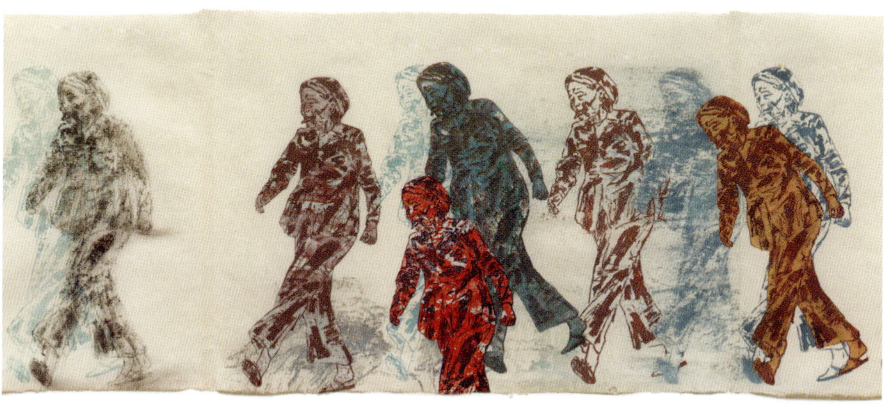

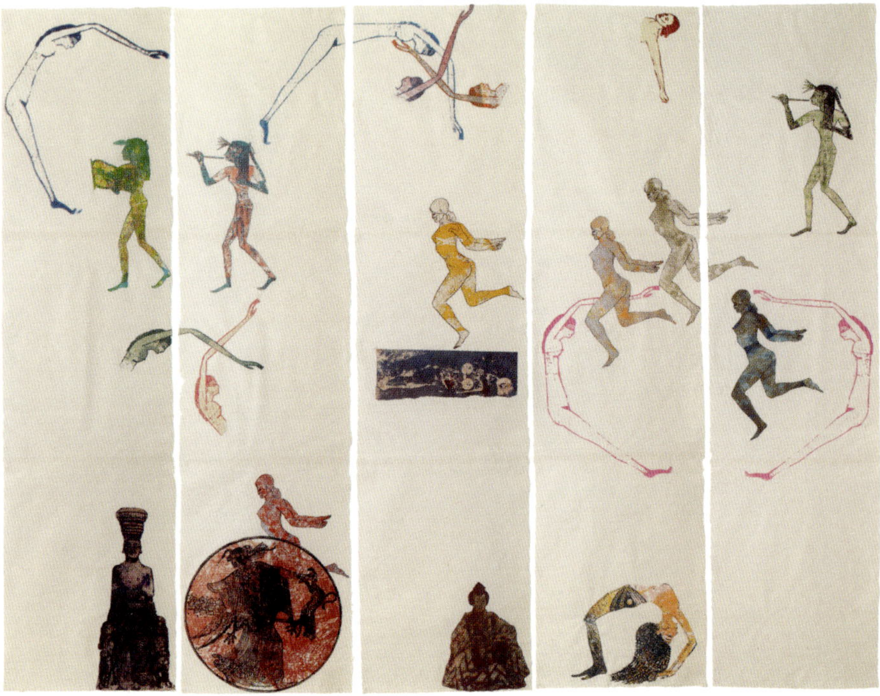

64
The Goddess Nut II, 1990
Handprinting and printed collage on paper,
overall: 213.4 × 279.4 cm (84 × 110 in.)

SFMOMA, San Francisco. Purchase, by exchange,
through a gift of Peggy Guggenheim
Photo courtesy Galerie Lelong, New York

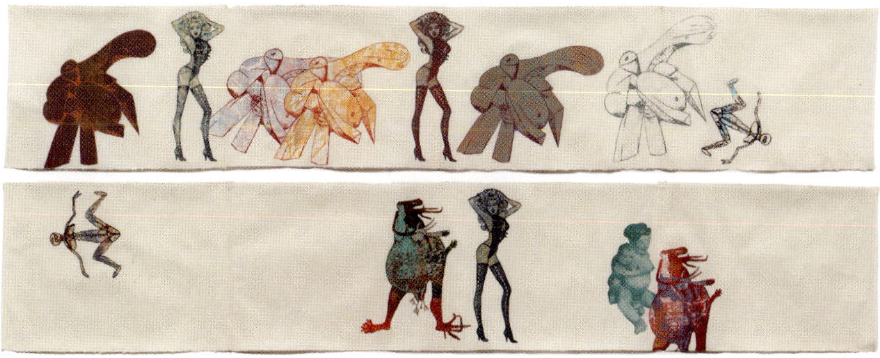

65
Picasso and Frederick's of Hollywood, 1990
Handprinted collage on paper, two parts, each:
43.8 × 278.1 cm (17 ¼ × 109 x in.)

The Nancy Spero and Leon Golub Foundation for the Arts
Photo courtesy Galerie Lelong, New York

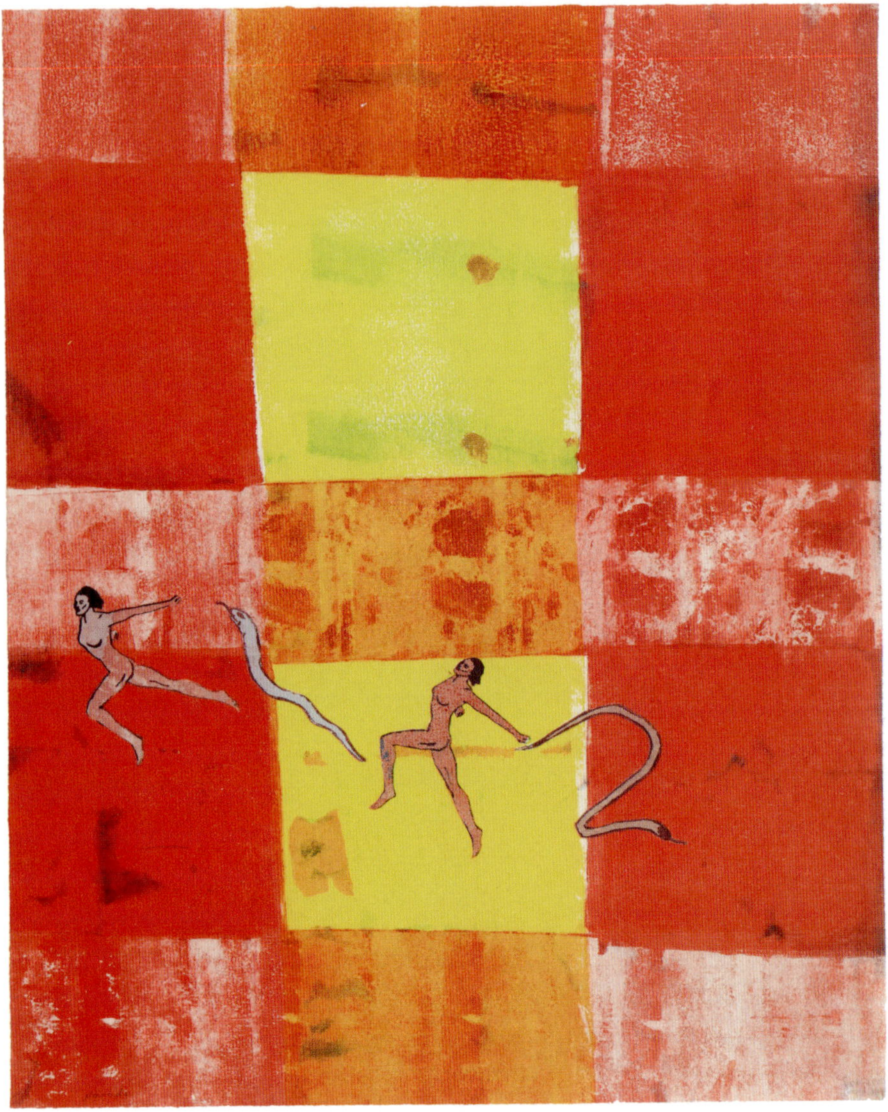

66
Parade, 1998
Silkscreen, 62.2 × 49.5 cm (24 ½ × 19 ½ in.)
Edition of 200

The Nancy Spero and Leon Golub Foundation for the Arts
Photo courtesy Galerie Lelong, New York

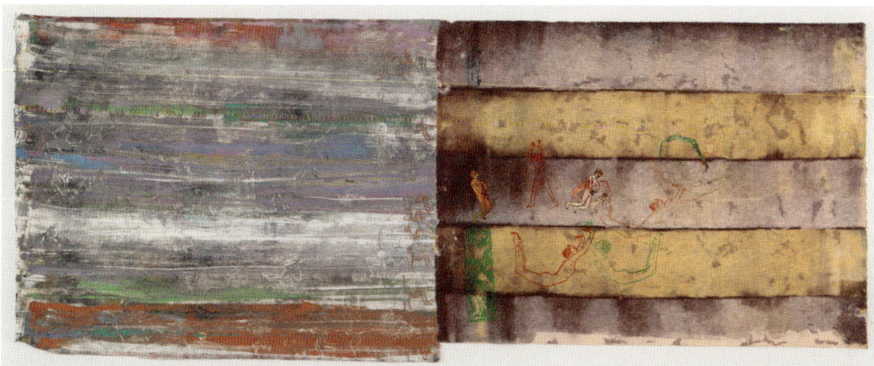

67
Frieze II, 2001
Handprinting and printed collage on paper, 51.4 × 126.4 cm (20 ¼ × 49 ¾ in.)

Private Collection
Photo courtesy Galerie Lelong, New York

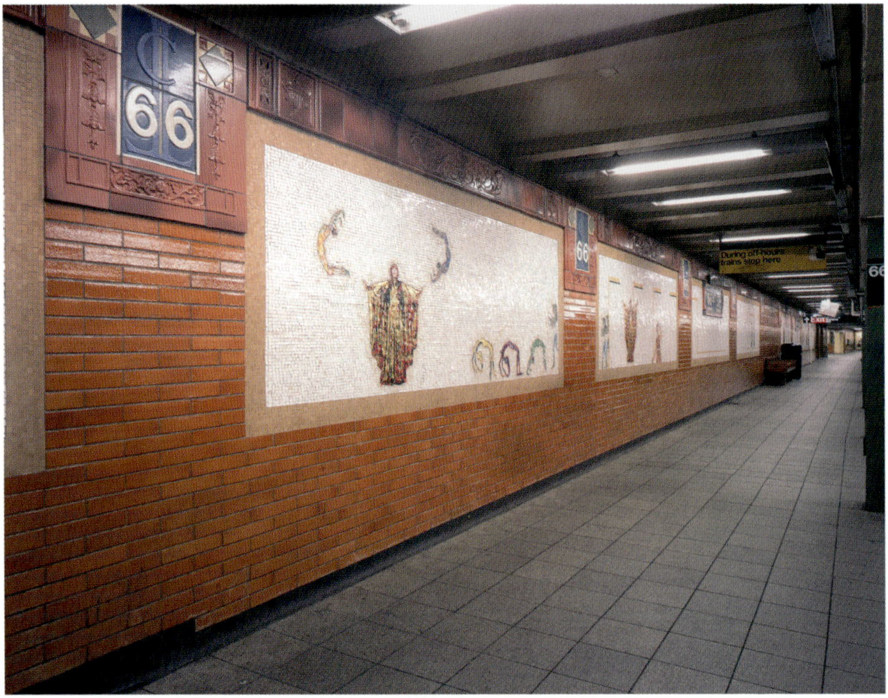

68
Artemis, Acrobats, Divas and Dancers, 2001 (detail)
Glass and ceramic mosaic

New York MTA (Metropolitan Transportation Authority), 66th Street Station
Photo courtesy Galerie Lelong, New York

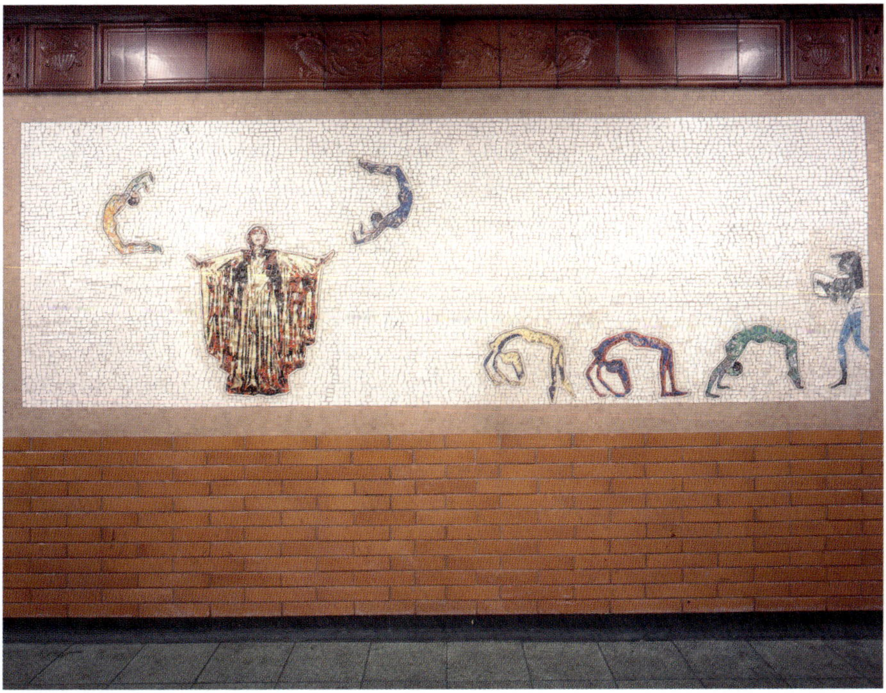

69
Artemis, Acrobats, Divas and Dancers, 2001 (detail)
Glass and ceramic mosaic

New York MTA (Metropolitan Transportation
Authority), 66th Street Station
Photo: David Reynolds. Courtesy The Nancy Spero
and Leon Golub Foundation for the Arts

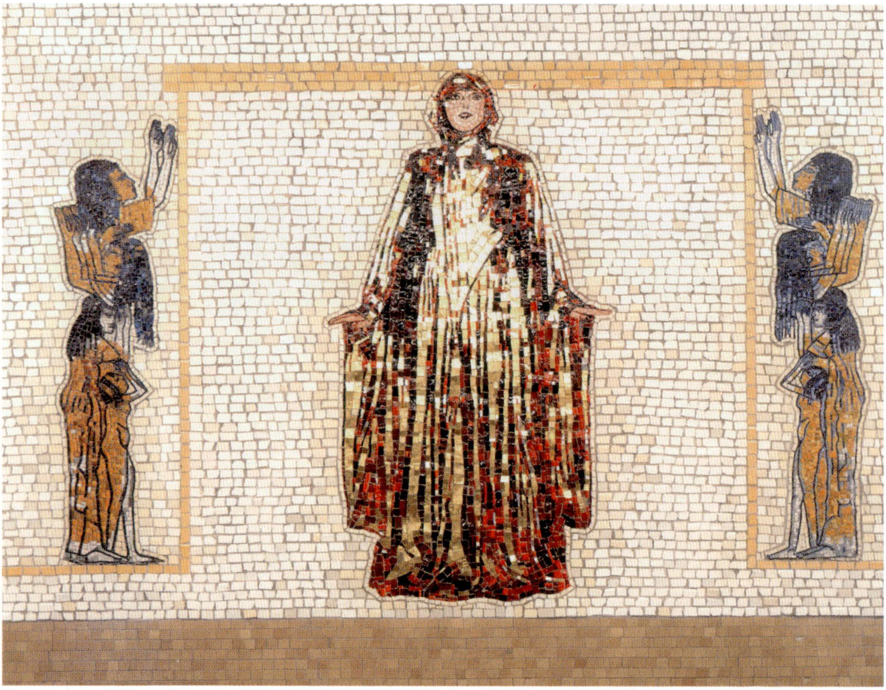

70
Artemis, Acrobats, Divas and Dancers, 2001 (detail)
Glass and ceramic mosaic

New York MTA (Metropolitan Transportation Authority), 66th Street Station
Photo: David Reynolds. Courtesy The Nancy Spero and Leon Golub Foundation for the Arts

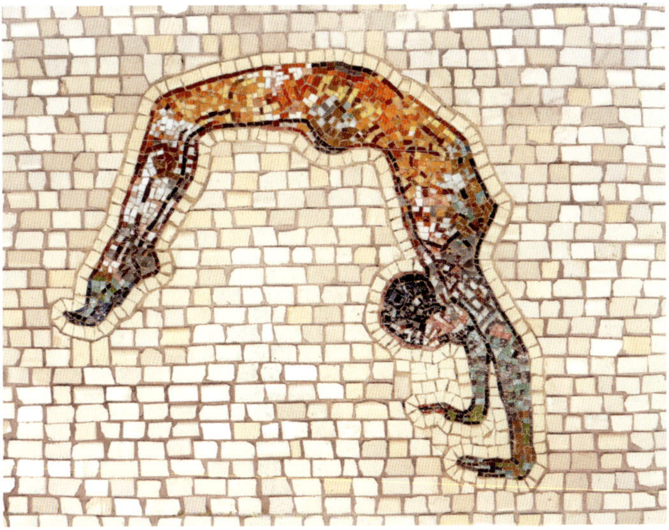

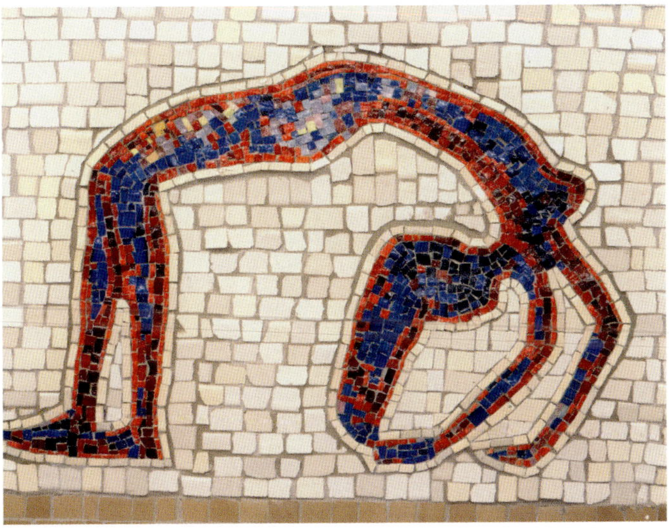

71, 72
Artemis, Acrobats, Divas and Dancers, 2001 (detail)
Glass and ceramic mosaic

New York MTA (Metropolitan Transportation Authority), 66th Street Station
Photo: David Reynolds. Courtesy The Nancy Spero and Leon Golub Foundation for the Arts

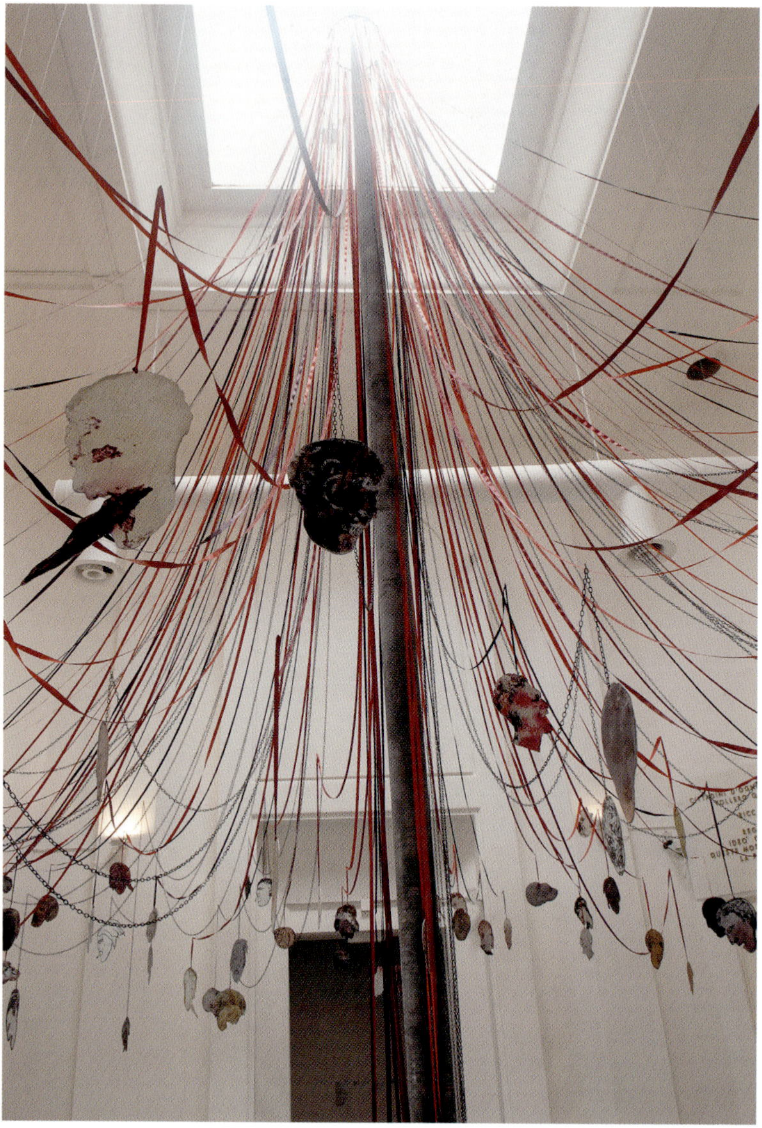

73
Maypole / Take No Prisoners, 2007
Handprinting on aluminum, ribbon, steel
chain, and aluminum pole with steel base,
1066.8 × 914.4 × 914.4 cm (35 × 30 × 30 ft.)
Installation view at the 52nd Venice Biennale, 2007

Photo: Giovanni Pancino. Courtesy Galerie Lelong

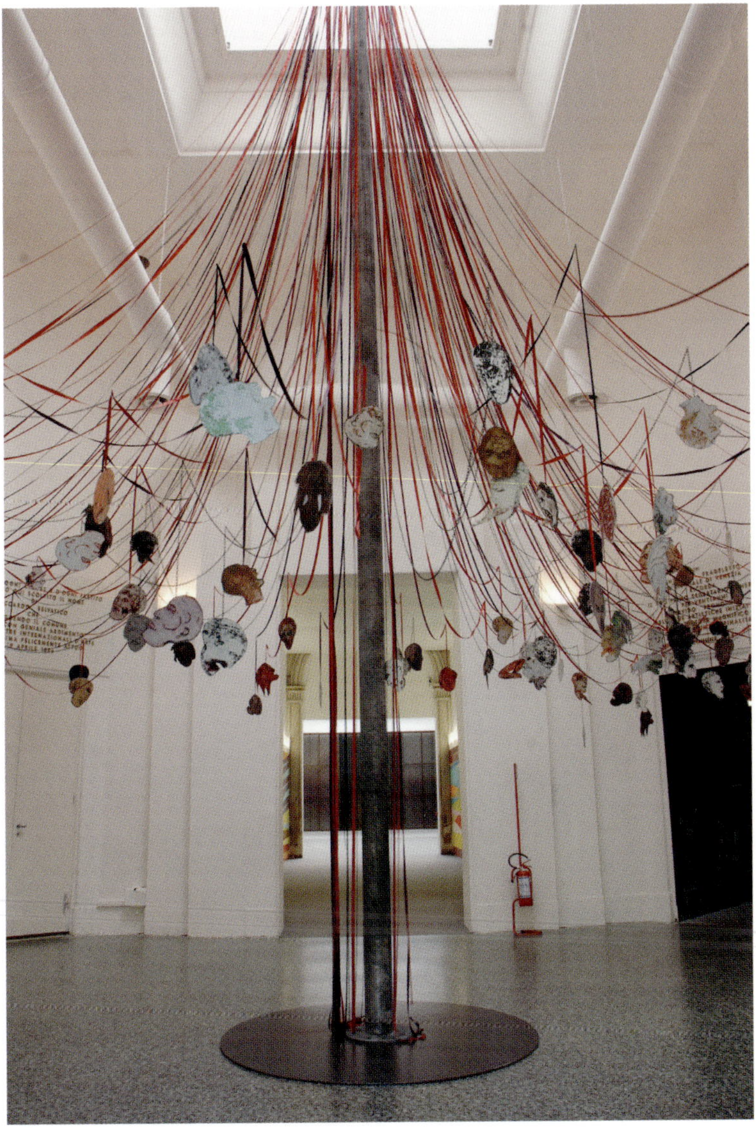

74
Maypole / Take No Prisoners, 2007
Handprinting on aluminum, ribbon, steel chain, and aluminum pole with steel base, 1066.8 × 914.4 × 914.4 cm (35 × 30 × 30 ft.)

Installation view at the 52nd Venice Biennale, 2007
Photo: Giorgio Zucchiatti. Courtesy Archivio Storico della Biennale di Venezia, ASAC

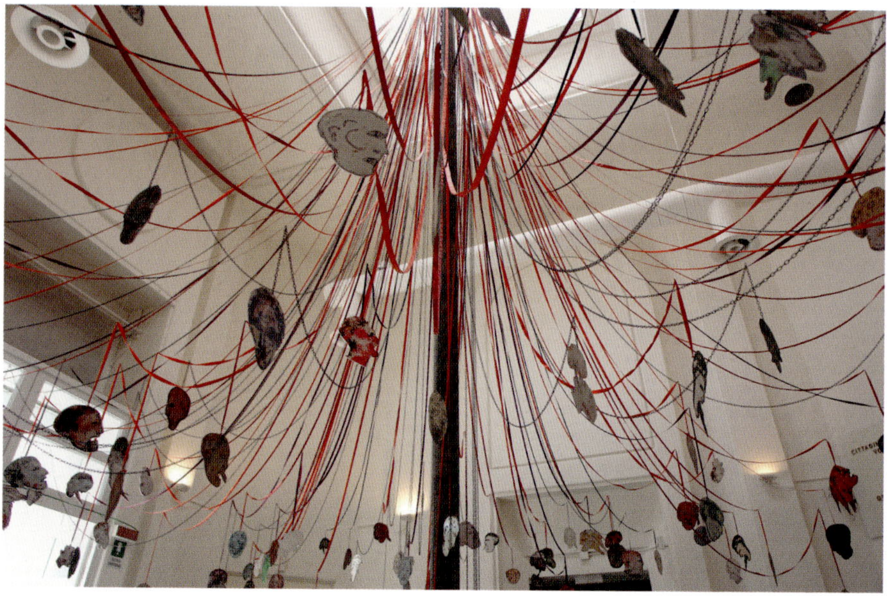

75
Maypole / Take No Prisoners, 2007
Handprinting on aluminum, ribbon, steel chain, and aluminum pole with steel base, 1066.8 × 914.4 × 914.4 cm (35 × 30 × 30 ft.)

Installation view at the 52nd Venice Biennale, 2007
Photo: Massimiliano Cadamuro. Courtesy Archivio Storico della Biennale di Venezia, ASAC

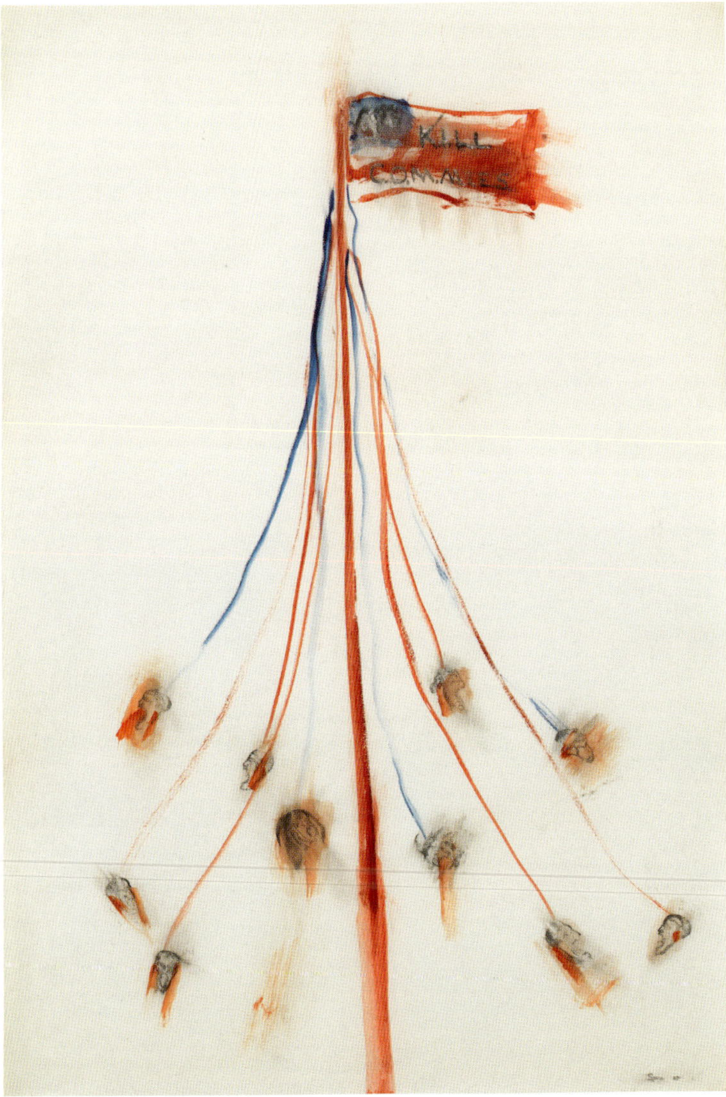

76
Kill Commies / Maypole, 1967
Gouache and ink on paper,
91.4 × 61 cm (36 × 24 in.)

Museum Folkwang, Essen
Photo courtesy Galerie Lelong, New York

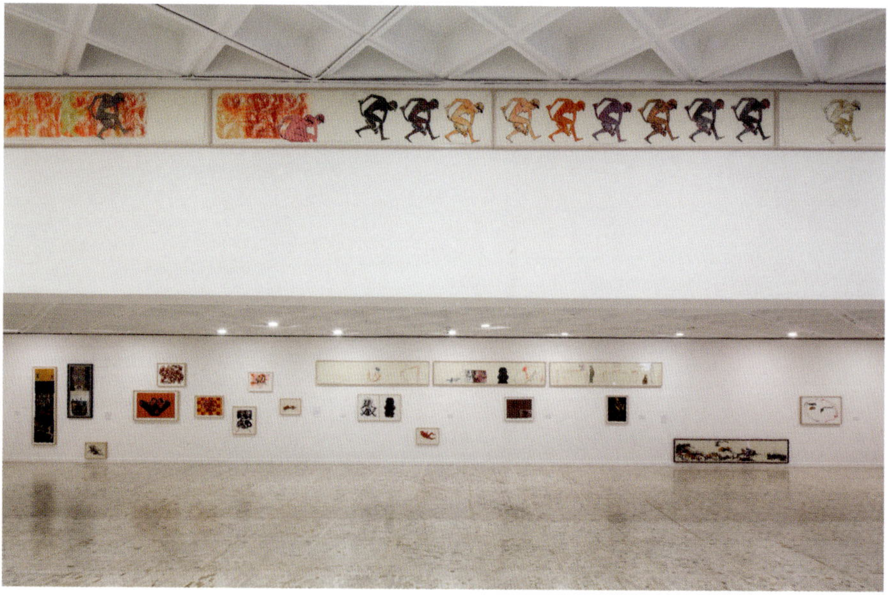

77
Installation view from *Nancy Spero: Paper Mirror*, Museo Tamayo, Mexico City, 6 October 2018 – 17 February 2019

Centro de Documentación Museo Tamayo

Author Biographies

Robert Storr is a curator, critic, and painter. From 1990 until 2002 he worked at The Museum of Modern Art in New York, where he was Curator and then Senior Curator in the Department of Painting and Sculpture. His exhibitions there included *Mapping*, *DIS*LOCATIONS, *Modern Art Despite Modernism*, and retrospectives of Robert Ryman, Tony Smith, Chuck Close, Gerhard Richter, Max Beckmann, and Elizabeth Murray. From 1990 to 2000 he directed MoMA's Projects program devoted to contemporary art, for which he organized small monographic shows by Art Spiegelman, Franz West, Tom Friedman, Ann Hamilton, and others. In 2002 he was named the first Rosalie Solow Professor of Modern Art at the Institute of Fine Arts, New York University where he taught through 2005. From 2006 to 2016 he served as the Stavros Niarchos Foundation Dean of the Yale University School of Art, where he continued to be a Professor of Painting through 2020. During that time, at the Yale University School of Art's 32 Edgewood Gallery he organized exhibitions on artists such as Francesco Clemente, Alex Katz, Jac Leirner, and Malcolm Morley, among others. Upon his retirement from Yale, he was named Dean Emeritus and Professor Emeritus of Art at the Yale University School of Art. In 2007 he served as Artistic Director of the Venice Biennale, the first American to hold that position. From 2015 to 2018 he was artistic director of the video art and performance festival of the Stavros Niarchos Foundation Cultural Center (SNFCC) in Athens.

Since 1982, his essays, reviews, and columns have appeared in *Art in America*, *ARTnews*, *Art Journal*, *Artforum*, *Art Press*, *Frieze*, *Parkett*, *Corriere della Sera*, and other magazines and journals. He is the author of numerous catalogues and books—notably of *Philip Guston: A Life Spent Painting* (2020) and *Intimate Geometries: The Life and Work of Louise Bourgeois* (2016). For the latter, he received the 2017 Filaf d'or Award, as well as the 2017 Filaf Award for Best Book on Contemporary Art. He has received honorary doctorates from the School of the Art Institute of Chicago, Swarthmore College, the University of the Arts London, and the Nova Scotia College of Art and Design, among other institutions. A frequent lecturer both in the United States and abroad, he has taught painting, drawing, art history, and criticism at numerous colleges, universities, and art schools. He is the recipient of prestigious awards for his criticism and curatorial work from organizations such as the International Association of Art Critics and the Archives of American Art. In 2016 he was awarded a fellowship from the John Simon Guggenheim Memorial Foundation. Made Chevalier des Arts et des Lettres by the French Ministry of Culture in 2000, he was subsequently promoted to Officier of the same order. Storr lives and works in Brooklyn, New York and New Haven, Connecticut.

Francesca Pietropaolo is an Italian-born art historian, curator, critic, and educator based in Venice. Her research interests focus on international contemporary art and on postwar European and American art. She has held curatorial positions at the Walker Art Center, Minneapolis; The Museum of Modern Art, New York; the Fondazione La Biennale di Venezia, Venice; and the Fondation Louis Vuitton, Paris. During her time at MoMA, she worked on *Roth Time: A Dieter Roth Retrospective* (2004), *Plane Image: A Brice Marden Retrospective* (2006), and exhibitions drawing from the museum's collection of works on paper. She was on the curatorial team of *Greater New York 2005*, MoMA/PS1, New York. At the Fondation Louis Vuitton, she was in charge of artist commissions, notably a site-specific installation by Ellsworth Kelly for the Auditorium, as well as works by Cerith Wyn Evans, Adrián Villar Rojas, and Taryn Simon, and she worked closely with artists such as Daniel Buren, Tomás Saraceno, Anthony McCall, and Lawrence Weiner. Her projects as independent curator include exhibitions such as *Wrinkles in Time* (IVAM, Valencia, 2009) and *North by New York: New Nordic Art* (American-Scandinavian Foundation, New York, 2011). At the Stavros Niarchos Foundation Cultural Center (SNFCC) in Athens, she co-curated the international video and film festival *Fireflies in the Night* (2015) and its second edition *Fireflies in the Night Take Wing* (2016), as well as the international program of performances *Only Connect!* (2017) and the video art exhibition *We Interrupt Regular Broadcasting to Bring You This Special Program!*

(2018). In 2019 she co-curated the exhibition *Artists Need to Create on the Same Scale that Society Has the Capacity to Destroy: Mare Nostrum*, an official Collateral Event of the 2019 Venice Biennale held at Chiesa delle Penitenti, Venice, and she co-organized its accompanying six-month interdisciplinary public program (including poetry readings, musical performances, public conversations, film screenings, and educational workshops). She is the curator of the retrospective exhibition *Francesco Clemente: In Between* for Triennale Milano (2026). She has lectured both in the United States and in Europe. She teaches at the Accademia di Belle Arti, Venice.

She is the editor of *Ellsworth Kelly*, first issue of "Les Cahiers de la Fondation" realized in collaboration with the artist (Fondation Louis Vuitton, Paris, 2014). She is the author of *Luisa Gardini* (De Luca Editore, Rome, 2016) and of numerous essays in publications for, among others, MoMA, the Walker Art Center, Fondation François Pinault, Kunsthaus Graz, Austria, the Estorick Collection, London, and Académie de France à Rome. She is the editor of *Interviews on Art*, the first collection of interviews with artists conducted by Robert Storr (HENI, London, 2017) and of the two-volume collection of his *Writings on Art* (HENI, London, 2020 and 2021). As critic, she has contributed to *Flash Art International*, *ARTnews*, *Art in America*, *The Brooklyn Rail*, *Art Press*, *Arte e Critica*, and the academic journal *Mediascapes*. She has interviewed artists such as Rosa Barba, Y. Z. Kami, Kapwani Kiwanga, Giuseppe Penone, Doris Salcedo, Haim Steinbach, and Tatiana Trouvé as well as composer Ludovico Einaudi and architect Jean Nouvel among others. She is editor at large at *The Brooklyn Rail*.

Acknowledgements

First and foremost, our heartfelt thanks go to Philip Golub and Paul Golub, and The Nancy Spero and Leon Golub Foundation for the Arts that they direct, for agreeing to participate in this endeavour and graciously allowing us to include reproductions of Nancy Spero's work in this volume. We are also grateful to Mary Sabbatino, Galerie Lelong, New York whose great help has been pivotal to the project. Moreover, at Galerie Lelong we sincerely thank Eve O'Brien for her assistance. Special thanks are due to the photographer David Reynolds, New York.

For their generous cooperation, our sincerest appreciation goes to the following individuals (in alphabetical order): Tobias Burg, Museum Folkwang, Essen; Michela Campagnolo, Archivio Storico della Biennale di Venezia, Venice; Kirsten Degel, Louisiana Museum of Modern Art, Humlebæk, Denmark; Lisa Dorin, Dan Byers, and Rachel Tassone, Williams College Museum of Art; Diana Freudl, Vancouver Art Gallery; Elaine D. Gustafson and Hannah Southern, Weatherspoon Art Museum, Greensboro, North Carolina; Jennifer Johns, Pennsylvania Academy of the Fine Arts, Philadelphia; Dennis Michael Jon, Minneapolis Institute of Art; Rosario Peiró Carrasco and Teresa López Flores, Museo Nacional Centro de Arte Reina Sofía, Madrid; Emily Putnam, National Gallery of Canada, Ottawa; Claudia Segura and Eric Jiménez, MACBA, Barcelona; Abril Zales, Museo Tamayo, Mexico City.

At HENI Publishing, we extend our warm thanks to Sarah McLaughlin, Production and Publications Manager, Sylvia Ugga, Book Designer, and Kirsty Watling, Editor, for their dedicated work at every step. Moreover, we owe special thanks to Rodney Hare, Director, HENI Publishing. To Joe Hage we express our unbounded gratitude for having believed in the *Focal Points* series project from its inception and for his unwavering commitment to make it possible.

Francesca Pietropaolo and Robert Storr

Index

0–10
9/11 terrorist attacks, New York (2001) 49

A
Abstract Expressionism 11, 17, 37
Abu Ghraib 14 fn.14
A.I.R. (Artists in Residence Gallery), New York 20
Algerian War (1954–62) 21, 54
Allende, Salvador 23 fn.6
Andre, Carl 17, 20
Angelou, Maya, *Still I Rise* 15 fn.16
anti-war movement 36, 37
appropriation 8, 14, 18, 22, 29, 36, 42 and fn.4, 44
Art in America 10
Art Brut 38
Art Institute of Chicago 10, 17, 19, 21, 38
Art Press 10
Art Workers Coalition 36
Artaud, Antonin 22, 24, 28, 39–40, 51 and fn.2
Artemis 8
Attie, Dotty 20
Ault, Julie 18
Aztecs 8, 20 fn.4

B
bande-dessinée (comic strips) 29
Barnett, Rick 21 fn.5
Bayeux Tapestry 8 fn.1, 22, 43
Beauvoir, Simone de
Le Deuxième Sexe 19
"Must We Burn Sade?" 28 and fn.1
Benjamin, Walter, *The Work of Art in the Age of Mechanical Reproduction* 23
Bernstein, Judith 20
Bhagavad-Gita 53
Borofsky, Jonathan 45 fn.5
Bourgeois, Louise 10
Brady, Mathew 49 and fn.1
British Museum, London 44

C
Calley, Lieutenant 36
Canada 17–18
Celts 23
The Center Show (exhibition, The Lesbian, Gay, Bisexual & Transgender Community Center) 21 and fn.5
Central America 21
Centre Georges Pompidou, Paris 18
Chicago 10, 19, 21, 38
Chile 23 and fn.6
civil rights movement 36, 37
Civil War 49
Cixous, Hélène 19
Cleveland, Ohio 19
collages 7, 18, 23, 28–29, 42 fn.4

Collection 1940s–1970s (exhibition, MoMA) **plates 38–40**
Conceptualism, Conceptualist 36–37
concrete poetry 30
Crimean War (1853–56) 49
Cubism 44
Cultural Revolution (China) 43

D
Dada 44
Darger, Henry 44
de Kooning, Willem 45 fn.5
deconstructionism 40
Derrida, Jacques 23, 29
Dickson, Jane 21 fn.5
digital animation, warfare 49–50
Dubuffet, Jean 38

E
Egyptian hieroglyphs 8, 42
Eichmann, Adolf 54
Eleey, Peter 18
Enlightenment 52
environmental sculpture 45 fn.5
Everson Museum of Art, Syracuse, New York 17–18, 34

F
feminism 7–8, 11, 18–19, 23, 27, 37–38
Field Museum of Natural History, Chicago 38
figurative paintings 11, 21, 37, 45
First World War 49
Formalism 36–37, 38
formats 43–45
France 21, 51, 54
Frederick's of Hollywood 14
Freud, Sigmund 30
Furies 53
Futurism 44

G
Galerie Lelong, New York and Paris 48, 54
General Idea 21 fn.5
Genet, Jean, *Notre-Dame-des-Fleurs* (Our Lady of the Flowers) 51
Golub, Leon 10, 13–14 fn.14, 19–21, 37
  Gigantomachies 37
Goya, Francisco
  Caprichos 42 fn.4
  Los desastres de la guerra (The Disasters of War) **plate 37**
  The Disasters of War 12, 52, 55
  Las mugeres dan valor (The Women Give Courage) **plate 37**
Graves, Nancy 10
Greece 8, 23
Greenberg, Clement 36
Guerilla Girls 21 fn.5
Guston, Philip 37

H
Haacke, Hans, *U.S. Isolation Box, Grenada 1983* 36
Haring, Keith 20 fn.4
Harpies 53
H.D., *Helen of Egypt* 8
Hinduism 53
Hiroshima 39, 53
history painting 23, 30–31
Hitler, Adolf 55
Holocaust 54

I
Indochina 54
Iraq War (2003–11) 13, 14 fn.14, 49
Irigaray, Luce 19
Irish Republican Army 42
Isaak, Jo Anna 20

J
Janus 53
Japan 55
Jews 54
Johnson, Lyndon B. 55
Joyce, James 31
The Judson Memorial Church, New York 21

K
Kahlo, Freda 38
Kali 53
Kaprow, Allan, *The Artist as Man of the World* 39
Kennedy, John F. 55
Kruger, Barbara 20 fn.4
Ku Klux Klan 37

L
LaChapelle, David 21 fn.5
Lascaux caves 30
The Lesbian and Gay Community Services Center, New York 21
Lidice, Czech Republic 54
Lincoln Center for the Performing Arts, New York 14
London 18
Lyon, Christopher 17

M
Madrid 18
Mao Zedong 43
Marx, Karl 30
Mendieta, Anna 20
"Messages to the Public" (video art program, displayed on Spectacolor advertising board at New York's Times Square) 20 fn.4
MeToo movement 14
Mexican muralists 38
Mexico City 18
Minimalism 17, 36–37
modernism 44
monsters 42 and fn.4
mosaics 14
mural paintings 7, 45
Murray, Elizabeth 10
Museo Reina Sofia, Madrid 18

Museo Rufino Tamayo, Mexico City 18 and fn.3; **plate 77**
Museum of Modern Art, New York 13, 18 and fn.3; **plates 38–40**
My Lai massacre (1968) 36, 54

N
Nagasaki 39
Nahas, Dominique 17
Nancy Spero: Paper Mirror (exhibition, Museo Tamayo) 18 fn.3; **plate 77**
Nancy Spero: The War Series (exhibition, Galerie Lelong) 12, 48
Nancy Spero: Works Since 1950 (exhibition, Everson Museum of Art) 11, 17–18, 34
Nancy Spero's Notes in Time (exhibition, MoMA) **plates 38–40**
Napoleon I, Emperor 52, 55
Nazis 54
Neel, Alice 10
Neo-Expressionism 20, 22, 28, 37, 43
New Museum, New York 17–18
New York 10, 17, 19–21, 27, 38–39
New York School 17, 19, 38, 45 fn.5
Newman, Barnett, *Lace Curtain for Mayor Daley* 36
Nixon, Richard 55

O
Oldenburg, Claes 17, 20
Oppenheimer, J. Robert 53

P
Paris 18, 19, 21–22, 38, 51
Parkett 9, 10–11, 26
Pentagon 39
Persian Lion Hunt reliefs 44
Petlin, Irving 20
Picasso, Pablo 14
La Baignade 14 fn.15
Pincus-Witten, Robert 20
Pinochet, General 23 and fn.6
Pollock, Jackson 45 fn.5
Pop Art 17, 38
Popular Science 49–50
postmodernism 27, 31, 51
Public Art Fund 20 fn.4

R
Rainer, Yvonne 10
Reagan, Ronald 21
Rivière, Jacques 40
Roman mythology 53
Rosenberg, Harold 37
Rothenberg, Susan 10
Rutgers University, New Jersey 21

S
Sahlman, Barbara 21 fn.5
Sandler, Barbara 21 fn.5
Schjeldahl, Peter 20

Schongauer, Martin,
The Temptations of Saint Anthony 42 fn.4
School of the Art Institute of Chicago (SAIC) 10, 17, 19, 21, 38
scrolls 7–8 and fn.1, 9, 22–23, 28–30, 43–44
Second World War 49, 54–55
Serpentine Gallery, London 18
Sheela na Gig 23
Shiva 53
Smith, David 45 fn.5
Southeast Asia 54, 55
Spain 52
Spectacolor 20 fn.4
Spero, Nancy **plates 18, 35**
Les Anges, Merde, Fuck You **plate 4**
Artaud Paintings 11, 12 fn.10, 41
Artaud Painting – All writing is pigshit **plate 26**
Artaud Painting – Formules de transformation **plate 23**
Artaud Painting – From this pain... **plate 22**
Artaud Painting – Les choses n'ont plus d'odeur **plate 27**
Artaud Painting – Then There Will Be... **plate 25**
Artemis, Acrobats, Divas and Dancers 14; **plates 68–72**
Black Paintings 11, 19, 38, 40–41
Bomb Shitting 53; **plate 13**
Les bourgeois passent... 51; **plate 21**
The Bug, Helicopter, Victim 53; **plate 8**
Clown and Helicopter 53; **plate 15**
Codex Artaud 11, 22, 29–30, 41, 51–52; **plate 35**
Codex Artaud I **plates 28–29**
Codex Artaud VI **plates 30–31**
Codex Artaud VII **plate 32**
Codex Artaud XIII **plate 34**
Codex Artaud XXV **plate 33**
Le Couple (Lovers) (1960) **plate 3**
Le Couple (Lovers) (1964) **plate 5**
Le Couple (Lovers VII) (1964) **plate 6**
Female Bomb 53; **plate 16**
Female Helicopters 53
The First Language 11, 41; **plates 55–56**
Frieze II 14; **plate 67**
Fuck 53
The Goddess Nut II 14; **plate 64**
The Great Mother **plate 2**
Gunship 53
Gunship and Victims 54
Helicopter and Victims 54; **plate 17**
Helicopter, Victim, Astronaut 54; **plate 19**

Homage to New York (I Do Not Challenge) 11; **plate 1**
Kill Commies / Maypole 13–14 and fn.14; **plate 76**
K.I.L.L F.O.R M.O.M 54; **plate 14**
Lovers **plate 7**
Male Bomb 52–53; **plates 9–11**
Male Bomb / Swastika 53
Maypole / Take No Prisoners 13–14 and fn.14, 24; **plates 73–75**
Me, Antonin Artaud, born September 4, 1896, out of a uterus I had nothing to do with **plate 24**
Mummified 38
Notes in Time 8, 11, 18, 23, 29; **plates 41–54**
Parade **plate 66**
P.E.A.C.E., Helicopter, Mother + Children **plate 20**
Picasso and Frederick's of Hollywood 14; **plate 65**
Sperm Bomb 52–53; **plate 12**
Torture in Chile **plate 36**
Torture of Women 42; **plates 57–60**
Torture of Women III **plate 61**
Victims Thrown From Helicopter 54
Vietnamese Women 11, 44; **plates 62–63**
War Painting **plate 18**
War Series 12 and fn.10, 22, 39, 50–51, 52–56; **plates 8–17**, 19–20
Star of David 53
structuralism 51
Suffragettes 19

T
terrorism 54
Think with the Senses / Feel with the Mind (exhibition, Venice Biennale) 12–13, 24
Times Square, New York 20 fn.4

V
van Bruggen, Coosje 20
Venice Biennale (2007) 12–13, 24
video games 50
Vietnam War (1955–75) 12, 21–22, 14 fn.14, 23, 36, 38–39, 50, 54–55
violence 8–9, 12, 14, 22, 28, 29, 50, 52–3, 55
Vollmer, Ruth 10

W
warfare 49–56
Wojnarowicz, David 20

Z
Zucker, Barbara 20

Focal Points

Volume 1: Bruce Nauman
Volume 2: Ad Reinhardt
Volume 3: Between a Rock and a Hard Place
Volume 4: Jasper Johns
Volume 5: Nancy Spero

Also by Robert Storr
(edited by Francesca Pietropaolo)

Interviews on Art
Writings on Art 1980–2005
Writings on Art 2006–2021